1374

THE PUBLISHED WORK OF PENSATIA
(Helen Merrick Bond)

A JOURNEY INTO THE LIGHT, Volume
One 1958
   The Door of the Heart, reprinted . . . . 1963 & 1973
   The Stone and Elixir, reprinted 1970
   The Inner Signature, reprinted 1977

THE MASTER H 1961
   The Master H, reprinted 1976
   The Flame of White, reprinted 1981
   The Rose of Life, reprinted 1981

THE HIGH MOUNTAIN 1965
   Reprinted 1978

THE LOTUS OF WISDOM 1968
   Master H's Call to Humanity
   The Disciple and the Master

A JOURNEY INTO THE LIGHT Volume
Two 1972
   Living Words From the Master
   The Path
   The Golden Dawn

VIGIL 1976

THE MAGNETIC LIGHT 1980

THE FLAME OF WHITE &
THE ROSE OF LIFE 1981

THE FLAME OF WHITE

&

THE ROSE OF LIFE

The Flame of White

&

The Rose of Life

By PENSATIA

THE EUCLID PUBLISHING COMPANY

New York

Library of Congress catalog Card No.

81-67515

Copyright 1961 & 1981
by Helen Merrick Bond

ISBN 0-935490-02-7

Contents

THE FLAME OF WHITE

PRELUDE

I Pensatia, humbly walk into the Flame of White, and in obedience to Love, from the crypt of the Flame of Wisdom, in the year of 1943, pen as I receive.

Open your heart, drink with me from the spiral of infinite flow. Ponder well the interior message given me from the inspiration of the infallible Masters who live in consciousness of the Flame of White.

Let us together thank God for the privilege granted me, for it is not I who write, but the "I Am" of my divinity.

Therefore, by the Seal of the Holy Dove, by the Eye of Akasha, and the Blessed Mary, I Pensatia, a student of the Rose, by the aid of the Master H, promise to write this book.

PENSATIA

THE FLAME OF WHITE

Dedicated to all who seek its Holy Essence.

Come, readers from all countries, students and disciples of the Rose, let me tell you of the most treasured experience on the Path: The glorious Light of the White Flame.

As I write immersed in it, peace and staying power flows through me. Heart and organs respond to their divine purpose. Love, co-breath of my soul, walks at my side.

Up to the Sanctuary of the Hierarchal Christus, the Flame Itself, I stand in the chalice of circular whiteness. Here, as one learns to stand still and cast aside all earthly garments, one may see. All that is, was and shall be is pictured within it.

All students of the Esoteric Path must attain consciousness in this Flame—seeing, hearing, and then come forth, obeying. All work of the Inner Rose is carried on from here.

"Well done, student," so speaks the Christus to all who enter the coil of white.

These are the words from Master H:

"The Flame of White holds the ever beating heart of Love, the nesting place of the 9th vibration, and the instant creation of all your divine and mortal seeking. It is the vibrating answer to every prayer, the supernal goal of every weary Pilgrim of the Path. All who reach the Flame of White and stand therein shall receive heaven, and earth as well. Thus it is written, and thus it will be.

"Let the whiteness of the light of the Flame cover you by day, and night; you then shall walk through all experiences, alive, healthy, a magi to bless and serve. You shall be fed, clothed, housed with the wealth of heaven and earth also. Wedded to Love, your bridegroom shall be finite and infinite.

"Give not up all who tread the Path, sever not allegiance to Lotus and the Rose. Fall you may, but ever arise

1

and climb up to the answer of Man's eternal quest. As one obeys, so shall one speak and bring forth. Air, Earth, Fire and Water shall obey and serve you. A comforter, a partaker of joy, sorrow, loss or gain; all will be equalized, transmuted in the Flame of White. Animals, life of the wild shall pay thee homage.

"At the shrine of Mastery, the absolute bloom of the Rose comes forth for the disciple. The Christus proclaims it, the Dove of the Heart sounds the gong. Mighty Ra cries: Hail to all who are regenerated in the Flame of White.

"Yes, Pilgrims of the Rose, this Flame of White is the prestige all have earned who enter. It is the end of the painful climb through the darkness of the bleeding discipline. Now the disciple has only to be still, reap and obey, thus penetrating the whiteness with one's inner senses. This is not painful as the preceding trials. For all who enter here have experienced the climactic cleavage of the centers, which gains them entrance into the Flame of White.

"To each in a different way does the cleavage take place. To some it comes with acute swiftness, often under the guise of illness. This climax is as lightning. It strikes swiftly, and in one full stroke breaks asunder the earthly chains of the sacred centers, lifting the disciple into his sublime initiation, while still in the body. If transition occurs, a glorious entrance in conscious illumination comes.

"That a battle must be fought . . . at this stage of development . . . is not denied by the Masters. By prayer, faith and utter reliance on the God of your heart—all will survive the inevitable cleavage, if one's mission calls for such.

"This quick climactic severing of the sacred centers spells quick destiny in the career of the student. He is lifted out of his old axis and is transmuted to a new dimension of being. Here in this high vibrational Flame, one must learn to use the awakened centers in sight, hearing and travel. Only with the utmost guidance from the Masters can one in safety learn to function with power and authority here. This Flame of White is the Inner School, the Inner Circle, of which the arduous foundation of the Path is for. . . . To some the cleavage is not so drastic. Neither is the attainment thereafter so complete. The greater the pain, the greater the gain. This does not imply that only those who suffer may find the Way. It does mean that the more pressure and effort the student gives, the more intense the cleavage—the more beautiful the Cosmic Illumination—and the greater the obligations and service thereafter.

"In the mild severance the psychic centers are opened by the aid of a Master. It seems partiality is shown. Yet not so. This grace comes by past cause and effect. Close contact with the Master has been in some incarnation. So now the disciple reaps the blessing when most needed.

"Remember, when this happens and with ease one passes the cleavage, a threefold obligation to use his powers in unselfish service becomes a must for the student. If he fails to work and learn in the White Flame all opportunity in the next life will be denied him. For cosmic law demands in receiving a spontaneous giving back to humanity.

"Those who by shock and pain bear the cleavage, the Master knows, they have learned that all gifts of heaven are only granted us to give back to others.

"There is a third way of admittance to the Flame. It is by the law of assumption. The Masters look into the records of the Word. They see the mission the pupil is to play in the service of the Rose. They perceive the student has exemplified the life of the Rose, borne the thorns with only love activating his every move. Almost the sacred centers open, but because of one great debt of the past the climactic cleavage cannot take place. It is now that the compassion and forgiveness of the Creator works. As

Christ forgave the penitent thief on the cross, so also does the Christus and the Masters on occasion, by the compelling vibrations of the pupil's penance, use the law of assumption and have the cleavage take place. By this gracious gesture of the Hierarchy, the disciple, devoid of pain, walks into the coil of Isis. Henceforth the love of his pure dedication bears example as, unafraid, he communes with the Masters and carries out their cosmic orders for universal service.

"So mark well, three methods only open the inner centers to the White Flame: The painful dynamic way; the aid of another Master or soul mate; or by the direct intervention of the Master. So sayeth the blood of the Rose. So sayeth I Master H. So is the Word. Here in the temple, here within the White Flame, are the glories of creation, the wisdom of God's heart, the endless library of cosmic dimensions. The exalted departed await in green pastures the presence of all students of the Path.

"Let us assume we have made the first baby step into the Flame of Flames. Let not its brightness frighten you. Know that it is peaceful and quieting. Its essence strengthening, healing and life giving. Just be still and drink in its whiteness with all thy interior body. Bathe daily in its white vibration. Listen for the voice of the Master. Obey what is said no matter how soft the voice . . . and ask what thy will in the Flame, the Master will answer. Believe no matter if all seems untrue when earth dimensions are resumed.

"Appearances often disarm the disciple when leaving the whiteness for the lesser, but remember, it is only the duality, the tempter saying 'believe not'. Smile, rejoice, say to all negative thought: begone in the name of Love and the Rose. Then go about your daily duties knowing all that transpires within the Flame shall be.

"When least expected, the objective realization will take place, when God speaks. When you hear 'The Gong has sounded' know the hour is at hand. Fulfillment, materially and spiritually can come in the twinkling of an eye. Whatever the Master asks of you, start and do; thus will the blessing of the Rose be yours.

"Now, Pensatia, you who pen from the Flame, I close this first chapter with the breath of the Logos sealing it, with the promise that all who seek shall find, and in finding enter, and in entering have."

I walked away from the Flame. Three angels stood by. "Blessings be on all who read," they spoke as one. Thus love encompassed me. Again they spoke: "We are the guardians of the whiteness of heaven. Eternally we live at the entrance of the inner circle in the Flame of White."

All who reach here ever sense the angels three. Thus they know they have trod where no earthly man enters.

chapter ☆☆ TWO

Master H speaks again from the Flame of White.

"Pensatia," and his voice sounded with all the keys of heaven and earth, "all disciples start at the base of the Flame and work up to its exalted summit. In this heavy whiteness of Mist of the Gods, the student stays until he can converse freely in the vibrational code of Isis. Step by step, as in his earthly lessons and discipline, so also begin his lessons and discipline in the inner school. As he obeys, learns and does, so will his ascent in the Flame be, until finally he and the Flame are wedded in eternal bliss and service.

"It is not easy for the student to stand on this new territory. It takes all the trust and faith of a true disciple of the Rose. For as in the outer, so also do the Masters test and try one in their early lessons in this inner school. Each

Master will put many appearances before the pupil. Almost it seems at times that all that has been told is a cruel mockery, a fantasy woven by the Devil himself. Now, if the student is well grounded, he knows without a doubt that these appearances are only tests, that in spite of all objective deceptions the words of the Master are infallible. All that is spoken in the Flame of White will be.

"Unless one has inner faith, one is apt to flounder. It is only this deep abiding faith in God and the Masters which carries one safely up and through the Flame of White to pure authoritative knowledge and power. No Master can give this essential attribute. It is the key all must create for themselves. This I do say: Bare-headed under the Fire of Isis, if one believes with faith and obeys in the inner circle, no matter if all seems lost, if all weakness of the past appears to sweep down upon one, if you look up with shining eyes and heart to the garment of the Christus, up to the All-Seeing Eye, up to the love of the Blessed Mother, your tests will pass, and lo, the Master shall say to you, 'Well done, servant of the Rose.'

"So soldiers of the Flame, stand still at the base of Isis, drink of the red, the white and the blue. Stand still and get thy balance. Remember the hand of 'we the Masters' hold in safety all students who persevere. The base is the fiery furnace, the disciple's last testing ground. Pass this threshold, otherwise you are belched back into the outer. By the right of endeavor your efforts alone have brought you to the first round of the inner court. Only by your efforts can you stay.

"It is an idle wish to assume that in entering the base henceforth your rating is assured. Alas! That it were true. Sad, but drastically so, many go back. The Flame of Isis is too great a challenge, a sacrifice. They long for the familiarity of lesser vibrations.

"Faith was too weak to continue in the spiral of consciousness of immortality. They look back and close the door. Yet because of their journey thus far, God is kind. Mercy and compassion will bless their departure. Yet, the luster, the Jewel of the Lotus, is hidden. The mundane curtain of darkness shrouds the departed evermore in this incarnation from entering the inner school.

"Of his own free will, thusly did the student choose. For as one chooses for the high so shall one's strength be. God and the Masters never fail us. We fail ourselves.

"In our agony we have only to cry, 'Master, Master,' and pray to God the Father. Always we are heard, strength is given."

chapter ☆☆ THREE

"Up, up in the misty whiteness of the Flame of White, step by step climbs the dauntless disciple. Every step mastered carries the student to new awareness of cosmic dimensions. It is only in quietness of mind, heart and body that ascension in the Inner Flame is possible. The higher one goes in consciousness the clearer the infinite becomes. All our inner senses respond. We hear, see and feel from our interiors. With loving care the Master reveals to the zealous student lesson after lesson of cosmic signature. Every degree of its technique is given the pupil until he is able to carry back in positive activity the wisdom of the fourth dimension and above.

"As one obeys he progresses into all the planes. A panorama of 'flood gates' open at will and the disciple now gazes in infinite strata. Departed loved ones, great souls who have passed transitions' initiation are now accessible. The barriers of earth vibrations are lifted. The student in positive freedom now lives in heaven even as he lives on earth. In entering the White Flame he has finished with the astral and enters into the spiritual. The Holy of Holies, the Chalice of the Grail, henceforth is his. Therein one may sip and quaff the nectar of the Gods.

"Travelers of the Way of Rose and Lotus, think not that this is an idle promise. Today as you read there are beloved disciples reaping this conscious immortality in the Flame of White. They have stepped within, passed their initiation by fire. Now indeed they sit at the feet of their Master.

" 'When the student is ready the Master will appear.' *Here* is where this saying becomes a reality. Remember, no matter how dimly one perceives in this esoteric Flame, all is inevitable and true. Only the reality is realized here. Often the Hierarchy cast appearances that seem to counteract the mandates of the Absolute. Remember this is only to test the pupil's integrity of will and purpose. So as a little child, let go of your mortal gage and with uplifted joy, walk through the clouds of earth deception. The Christus shall lay within your hands all that is ordained for you.

"The technique of the Flame of White interferes in no way with mundane affairs. No seclusion, in common parlance, is needed. The disciple now, anytime, anywhere with open eyes, may enter the cosmic dimension. This profound door of illumination opens by the touch of the golden key built by the long discipline of the Way. Now the Christus, Masters, the God of all peoples welcome and give him the Kingdom."

The words of this third chapter are sealed by the hand of Master H himself. The All-Seeing Eye bears witness to the Pen of the Word.

I Pensatia, only the amanuensis of the vigil, pray for strength to ever ascend into the whiteness of the Flame. And may strength be given all who read to choose aright.

"Love is the essence of the Flame of White. Until it is experienced on the Path, one is not ready for the climactic cleavage and entrance.

"Nothing save Love, forgiving, compassionate, Christ-like can prepare the way to Isis' Light. Let us seek therefore to eliminate hate, envy, jealousy, competition, ambition, self-ego-power and turn our heart to Rose and Cross, bear and transmute *all* in Love. Else all travel esoterically is of no avail. Love only can lift karma and bear one up and beyond the cross to God and the Masters. All attributes are nothing without this cosmic vibration. It must become a living part of the pupil before he dares ever knock at the inner gate.

"Love is the final touch to the Key to the Light of Egypt. It must color the aura of every student of the White Brethren. Through pain, sorrow, loss, darkness and crucifixion, Love is fertilized and brought to bloom. At its awaking the heart opens. Then the student is truly on the way to Love's altar in the Flame of White and the supreme initiation.

"No one but God and the Masters know when love has reached the point of cleavage into the Lotus. Remember this, disciples-to-be. When you make obeisance to this Light, when the great initiation takes place, and you pass the angels three, you will know without a doubt that Love alone brought you there.

"As you climb the Stair of Flame, love will guide you. In fact you are love and love is you. So will love of one and many be granted all who attain this mandate.

"That which is no longer ours shall pass from us, that which bears our inner signature shall come quickly to the waiting, worthy heart. All who abide in the Flame of White shall reap perfect self expression and their divine destiny.

9

"So be faithful, dare to stand still and obey the Inner Flame. So will Heaven serve you in fullness and power. All the wonders celestial will be bequeathed to you. All will be clothed with the Cloth of Gold, the Magi's Robe, the Wand of Moses. The Staff of Light, Life and Love will be given all to use for humanity."

chapter ☆☆ FIVE

Again spoke Master H from the Flame of White:

"I will now discuss seeing in the spiritual focus of the Gods. Very few, if any, see distinctly when first entering the Hall of White. Sense and feeling—a certain inner awareness supercedes sight for the time being. The student must first get his walking legs steady before the 'sights' of the Gods are open for him.

"Here as in the outer school the student must work, and do spiritual exercises given him by the Master for the use of his inner eye. For though the cleavage has taken place he is as it were a new born babe in an ethereal plane of reality. Therefore, time must be spent learning to adapt the esoteric eye, that it may pierce the brightness and behold the unending pictures of the Word.

"Slowly, as the disciple obeys and uses his eye of Shiva, daily he learns to see as clearly in the White Flame as in earth vibrations. Little by little the Master, according to the disciple's inner strength, takes him higher into the realm of the inner circle, and aids him to penetrate through the brilliant mist of ever circling white.

"As one learns to 'see', so must he be able to discriminate and learn all the signatures of heavenly objects. Here as in the outer school love only gives power to behold, know and find. The prayer of the heart is mighty and toilsome here. It stirs the Word to active giving to the student.

"All pure desires find realization under the gaze of Isis. At first faintly, like a gossamer etching, objects, people, scenery and writing comes before the inner eye. But if patient, obedient and studious to that so delicately perceived, soon the disciple will notice progress. Keener and more graphic will become his sight. There will come the hour when all the glory of cosmic vision will be his. 'The Voice of the Silence' will be as readable as the earth pages. Thy Master will reveal himself in the clear virile presence of his immortality. Thy cleavage has taken place, all thy centers are quivering, as a race horse well trained ready to start for the final race of attainment. Thy God and Master who hold the reins will surely ride you to victory. Like a horse who pulls for his master, so pupil, ride the white horse through the Flame of White to Shangri-la and the flower of the 9th vibration.

"Yet do not try to see too rapidly in the higher dimension. Let the White Chalice of the Grail give of its light to thee. As a child, be spontaneous, full of faith and expectancy. Believe all the Master reveals, no matter how faint. For if you do not believe when the sight is dim, if you do not embrace what is shown you, then vision will not expand and clear sight is denied you. So study what is given you and in some manner take its value back to earth and give out to all who come across thy path.

"Now in closing the 5th chapter let it be known that the gentle love of the Christus forms the circle of protection to all who enter herein. He is the Good Shepherd, you are His flock. The Rose and the Flame, the inner school, is the inner wire which connects one with cosmic consciousness. 'Knock and it shall be opened unto you' . . . 'Ask what you will, it will be.' So speaks the Master of Masters. So echo all the Masters in White."

chapter ☆ SIX

"Come, Pensatia," spoke Master H out of the Flame of White. "Let me show you the waters of life, flowing eternally. Be not afraid; just follow me," he directed.

With awe and wonder I obeyed. . . . Higher and higher we climbed in consciousness, getting closer to the center of whiteness. The Master seemed to propel me upward and forward. I realized that it was only through his aid that I traveled in so high a vibration.

On either side beautiful scenery of mountains, meadows and valleys were visible, changing with rapidity. Friendly, happy people were at ease. Colorful birds flew from bright green trees. Animals of many species ran and played through the countryside.

Higher we climbed, or ascended. Now and then I caught a glimpse of people I had known on earth . . . We ascended still higher, always in spiral form . . . Suddenly a host of angels bore down upon us. Each played a musical instrument which blended into an immortal symphony. Then it was Master H pulled me back and bade me be still and look.

A rush of silver waters came coursing through the center of White Flame. Power, vivifying, purifying and electrified swirled in mighty current through and around it until it was lost in a dazzle of golden light brighter than the sun.

I looked. Master H bent forward and did speak a word in the name of love, and behold! the waters were calm as a still mirror and wide as a margin of flat ribbon. He cupped his hands, did drink and bade me do likewise. He spoke: "He who sees and stands still and drinks of this shall have everlasting life, have access to all knowledge and power. All students who enter the inner school and stay, shall, must and will drink of the waters of life.

12

"By the use of the law of love they still the currents and can drink and bathe in its stream at will in safety. By the law of attraction love obeys love, and love, the vivifying essence of the waters, obeys always the call of love. Here in the waters of life, when prepared, the disciples bathe, drink and look into the cosmic waters for the reflection of the mandates from heaven which are pictured therein. Here, to all in a different way, Baptism takes place: the coming of the Holy Ghost, the Alchemical Marriage, the descent of the Doves of Heaven. When this transpires the student becomes a true disciple of the Master.

"Until these initiations are realized by the student, God and the Masters know, he cannot be trusted fully to carry out his earthly mission. Harken now to this infallible mandate embedded forever in the Fire of Isis: 'All students who embrace the waters of life, they who are Baptized in its current, they who meet the 'Bridegroom' shall have the power and authority to start, do and carry out their mission in life.' They will be told and given their orders. The Masters know they will obey to the nth degree. No matter how hard the task, or long, humble, strange or famous, the disciple will carry through and be silent.

"So students of the inner circle, when thou comest from thy Holy Baptism, rest in the Lord, let go and await word from the Master. Within the time of three, new orders will come.

"Let thy experience meanwhile mellow into serene exultation. Let thy prayers be in the heart, that sacred entrance to the corridor of the illumined. Live naturally, enter the table of the Christus, and in some three, your orders will come."

chapter ☆☆ SEVEN

"Write today, Pensatia, of the Sun of the Absolute," dictated Master H from the banks of the Waters of Life.

"Look," he said, pointing upward at that circle of golden light of which the physical sun is a reflection. "Here in the inner school the disciples strengthen and utilize their awakened interiors, until step by step they climb the circular stairway of the Rose leading to the citadel of pure Gold of the Hidden One. As they obey and carry out their orders they ascend into the Flame of White. Thus one is able to approach the golden disc, the splendor of the God of Gods.

"No disciple or mortal master ever drank from the heart of the Gold. Up, up to the golden rays they can and do reach the esoteric tower, lit by the Sun of the Absolute for the beloved disciples and Masters alone.

"Here all who are ready gather at the sound of the cosmic gong and bathe in the gold even as they have bathed in the white, the silver blue and the red. This is the highest round, the ultimate of mortal endeavor, while living in earthly body. No one may go beyond the golden light into the Gold Itself. This is the privilege, the grace of those of and beyond the Third Degree of Christ and the Buddha, the Degree of Perfection, of absorption into the golden heart of the Creator.

"The Third Degree is the nearest one may attain in mortal body. Very rarely and of his own choice does a disciple choose to go beyond the Third. For if so all human ties must be severed. Alone one must ascend to the Disc of Ra.

"The preceding Degree is as important as the Third and beyond. Either way the disciple chooses is to the glory of God and the Masters. Often, karma and one's mission call for the human ties of marriage and children. If in the past incarnation a marriage has not been experienced in

14

its innate beauty, then one must master and transmute such into its esoteric fulfillment, else one can not and dare not choose a higher altitude of service. Only under the law of cause and effect can the disciple choose.

"Obedience to spiritual law and to the Master's orders is imperative. When disciples have passed in victory the lesser degrees of the inner circle, then, and only then are they eligible to aspire to the greater role, that of ascension into the Gold of the Absolute. After once choosing, only as Christ Rays or in Bodies of Light do they migrate to earth vibrations. Never do they assume earth bodies again. Lesser Masters have that power. But the super signature of the Absolute has no earthly mandates, no earthly wires. Henceforth they who choose and are accepted are absorbed, or Masters of the Hierarchy of the Cosmic Host. All other masters, adepts, disciples may reach up in purity of heart and catch the words of wisdom which ever beam in spiral radiation from the Gold through the Flame of White.

"It is from this reservoir of the Cosmic Hierarchy that the laws of the Cosmos flow forth, and the mirror of Akasha was formed. Here the creative Waters of Life gush from the heart of the King of Kings. With scepter of dazzling love, in justice and power does the Eye of Shiva look down and see all. From the Creator's beat goes forth the gong for all acts of earth. Birth, marriage, death, all major climaxes, changes, opportunities, open and closed doors, happen only when the gong of Heaven sounds. Down, down through the spiral of white does the strike of the gong sound and echo to earth. Only to disciples is it a conscious occasion. To those not Cosmically aware, they speak of fate or luck. Yet the disciple knows all is self-made cause and effect, and by love's initiation only does the gong ring out from the Disc of Golden Flame. They know at each sound, the Infinite is speaking, saying: 'It shall be.'

"Sometimes the disciple's inner hearing is not yet keen enough. Then the Master relays the message, or fiat of the Word, and why it sounds. Remember this, always when the gong sounds, the time has arrived for certain things to come to pass in one's earthly life. At that moment, from the first strike of the gong, that which is conceived 'within' slips into objective birth. When a Master tells you the gong has sounded, and this or that will be, know, and with steadfast faith wait and behold the 'fruit of the Path.' Even as Solomon stated, 'There is a time for everything.' In the Flame of White each student realizes the infinite truth of this saying. For the Wheel of Birth, of action and reaction, is revealed.

"One knows the mathematical certainty of spiritual law. Everything is by law and order. Supreme justice prevails. When certain vibrational keys are struck all comes to pass. Vibrating to that note nothing may be forced—if so it crumbles. Only what is earned and written 'self-made' in the Scroll of Gold comes forth.

"When the Word went out the divine destiny of all mankind also became law. In minute degree every act and thought that has been and will be is etched in God's sacred heart. The whole only God knows and They absorbed in Gold. The lesser Masters, (only lesser because they are not fully absorbed in the Absolute), they, as God permits, are shown the destiny of every pupil. All their work with the disciples is to hasten the sounding of the gong.

"If it were not for the age-old Path of the Masters, countless ages would pass before humanity made any progress. . . . Rejoice esoteric disciples. Every prick and pain, every nail of negative karma transmuted, makes nearer the hour when the Cosmic Gong shall strike. Thus bringing to pass all the Masters' words and that which is written divinely for each man and woman. This is not blind fate, but the divine design coming forth—beautiful, uplifting, free, containing only love and joy.

"Everyone has freedom to choose, to go with their divine scroll, or away from it. As we decide we make our own fate. Either it is in harmony with God's mandate, or else we create negative pictures into Akasha. Then only by tears, loss, tragedy, their divine mission and heritage is darkened. Through self-made karma one has to unweave the wrong threads we ourselves have sown into the bloom of life."

chapter ☆☆ EIGHT

Up through the Flame of White to the Waters of Life; on through its majestic sweep, Master H guided me to the lofty summit of the mount of illumination. "Come," he said, "seat yourself on this snowy whiteness of altitude. Write as I picture the essence of all wisdom.

"Here is the mount of Cosmic Consciousness. Here, all disciples must abide before the star of authority is blazed in indelible fire upon their foreheads. Its cool, clear atmosphere must be breathed and absorbed. Its foursquare scenic splendor all students esoteric must perceive and understand. The true vision of divinity is revealed on the mountain top of the Illuminati. Here the ultimate of the Absolute is thundered in mighty notes to the disciple. In naked white light with bared head the disciple looks up as he stands upon the awe inspiring mountain top of illumination. God seems to step down. His words sound forth on the holy mountain infallible mandates from the Cosmic Hierarchy.

"Alone, except for the Master, the disciple walks and studies in the brilliant letters of his orders. He rests and partakes of the manna of the Masters. At last 'Home' is found in the abode of the White Brethren. Shangri-la is open house to the disciple's feet. He is a privileged comer and goer of every part and parcel of that august place.

"Until one is able to ascend this mountain the Master never reveals himself in complete regalia. On this citadel Cosmic Initiation for every disciple takes place at the appointed moment. Power is given the ready disciple. He has blazed through the crucibles and transmuted base elements in the Flame. Now the great initiation in the 'Air' of the afflatus of the zenith of illumination is his.

"Not until all lesser initiations take place can this climax happen. To reach the lofty altar of Isis one must have left behind all earth vibrations. The Path will see to that. Until one has and gives up, until one has not and receives, until joy and sorrow both have embraced one, the student is not ready, and never can be. Rest assured, before the veil of the mount is lifted, and you are called to climb its high spiral to the supreme initiation of all, you will have supped of ecstasy and drank of earth sorrow. You will have known the gold of earth and are ready for the gold of heaven.

"Let us assume," continued Master H, "by right of conquest the student has arrived at this momentous mount of awareness, where he lives in the aura of the Hierarchal Host. Here the grueling vibrations of earth do not exist. The rare companionship of Master and disciple is a conscious reality here. The inner commands now and changes all outer weakness into strength and beauty. On this sacred esoteric mountain the disciple is capable in ever greater degrees of holding the Light of Isis. The purified air pours upon him until his inner and outer pair and become impregnated with its potent flame.

"It is a grace and privilege, this sojourn on the mount of illumination. There in the snows of its summit the Master prepares the disciple for the dynamic birth of all his powers, interior and exterior. If the initiation here is finished—one becomes a magi, ripe for lesser mastership, or greater. On this mountain top all rituals and outer lessons are eliminated. First-hand the disciple receives and studies from the Master and the cosmic archives. No barriers exist. The Master hears and answers the pupil and instructs.

"It is this tutelage on the mountain top which is the flowering of all the preceding steps on the Wisdom Path. It is the crowning diploma of all the student's efforts on the Way of the Rose. In the white bracing air of the White Brethren and the immortal beams from the Eye of the Hidden One, each disciple sits at the feet of his beloved Master, learns, obeys and grows into his holy initiation sublime.

"Often, a long time, perhaps several incarnations must pass before here on the summit the Royal Signature of the Illuminati is earned. Yet it is possible, and there are students, and will be again, those who receive the 'Mark of Isis' in this incarnation. How long it takes depends on the zeal, obedience and unselfish love of each disciple. Is the pupil willing to pledge still a part of every day to the tasks given by the Master? . . . Remember, now the tempter seeks to divorce the aspirant from his culminating victory. A duplicate of the Dark Night overwhelms the heart and endeavors to persuade the disciple that the mount of illumination is not for him.

"Know O seekers of the Keys of Life, if faithful to God and the Masters, the duality of all temptations will not avail. Here in the eternal snows of the flute of Ra your victory is assured. The Masters infallible hold in escrow the secret jewel of attainment. They lay with their hands the esoteric brand upon the forehead of every initiate who has come through the Holy Trial and Air of the Mount.

"Many false orders come at this stage of soul evolution. Almost one will believe it is the Master's will to do thus and thus. Yet remember, in prayer and meditation one will know the real. At this time some may feel they are doing nothing for humanity. Yet such is not true. O disciples, obey the inner mandates in the heart. There only will the Master speak true. Obey all that is given at the beginning, as no new orders will be until you have fulfilled the old.

"Here in the inner school law and order prevails. Obedience must precede all other objectives. Know also if a Master decrees a thing it will be. So at this epochal cycle on the Rosy Path forbear thy earthly work. Know now is the crucial period when your cosmic destiny is at hand. Just as you are able to stand in the Flame of White, the Christus and the Masters are preparing each and every one.

"Faint not when all the Master says seems not to come at the appointed moment. Remember, until the disciple's faith is without a doubt, and unshakable, nothing will objectify. So in the darkness of the Path, at all stages and times keep your faith burning as a lamp of heaven. Let no finite conception or deception mar thy faith in thy Master's words spoken from the inner circle in the swirling Flame of White.

"Know always the Master's love surrounds you. Ask now what you will—it shall be granted you, be it of earth or heaven. Do not hesitate to voice thy desires, even though they are already known. Yet it is the law, one must ask. Remember Christ's words: 'Seek first the Kingdom of Heaven and all else will be given you.' "

chapter ✩ N I N E

"Write, Pensatia, of the Golden Flame," spoke Master H standing in the whiteness of the Mountain Top.

"As the disciple sojourns here, at the appointed time he is told to bathe in the Flame of Gold that showers from the Absolute Itself. Not until the student has attained the basic technique and absorbed the white light is it possible to walk under and drink of the golden strength of this essence of regeneration, the overflow of the Creator's Love. To be worthy to bathe in its dazzling rays is to know one's self-conscious state of divinity.

"Daily contact with the Gold burns the final signature of Isis on the heart of every disciple. Herein is the secret of the Rosy Cross revealed. This happens when in dedication we lay ourselves upon the altar for God's use and service.

"The first step into the Gold acquaints one with the stir of God speaking direct to soul of man. It is the true court of justice, law and mercy. Here under the majesty of its rays the disciple enters his final crucible, only this time it is a crucible of the fourth dimension, a crucible of the glory of God pouring down upon those disciples who work, pray and obey in the Golden Flame. It is the crucible which brings expression to the now awakened centers. To be allowed to bathe in its splendor spells health and vitality.

"No Master bids a disciple enter this Flame of Gold unless regeneration is decreed for the physical body. When one enters the 'Golden Shower' one's passports are assured. Health of mind and body is and will be no matter how deceptive outer symptoms and appearances. You are *whole* in the Flame. Remember, you need naught but divine meditation now. Accept that and know all else will be added as needed. No Master would dare open the spiral of Gold unless one was ready. This bath accentuates and increases one's earthly life. It makes visible the Master and brings speech and creative power to all thy interiors. The love and fruitage of the soul comes forth. Pray within its eternal wisdom and great and swift will be thy answers, disciples of the Rose.

"This Flame of Gold is the loving breath of the Good

Shepherd, the Father's benediction. It is the glory after the travail. To walk in its love rays will transmute the lesser into the higher, all weakness into strength, ugliness into divine beauty. Here the prodigal returns to the 'Fatted Calf', all that the Father has is his for the asking. Celestial music breaks forth for his inner ears, the flute of Ra plays the notes of Mastery. The All-Seeing Eye looks down through the Golden Flame and says: 'Fear not, my beloved disciple, you have sought the Kingdom of Heaven first, all else shall be added. Be happy and of good cheer. Walk, obey the Master's voice and great and long will be thy life and service on earth for thy brothers of all races.'

"This is the last purifying Flame, which separates all dross, and leaves one born in the essence of Gold. So continue to stay in its eternal vibrations, and fear not if at the beginning the stay is trying. Only know, if told to enter, you will triumph with victory regardless of all appearance of sickness. For often the student feels symptoms of illness—yet he will not succumb. It is only the Gold working out the dross.

"Call 'Master, Master' . . . yet stay bravely in the Golden Flame. Nothing of harm can happen—neither mind or body will be ill. For as said before: No one enters the Flame of Gold until ready to stand its potent power. So make oneself at home, in long or short intervals it matters not, for God and the Masters watch thy every move. They will not fail you. By your obedient effort you have entered. You will be sustained. Your illumination is promised.

"Have you asked for anything? Know already it is yours. Give thanks, for in the Flame of Gold, like a miracle when you least expect, all desires of the heart are granted the worthy disciple."

"High up in the center of this Gold," continued the Master H, "is the Altar of Altars where, in prostrate supplication, the disciple prays for the grace of the Most High to flood his consciousness with Light, Life and Love, to use for the evolvement of darkness and ignorance.

"All disciples who kneel in consciousness, or stand at the Altar of the Inner Rose of the Golden Dawn, shall receive the grace of the Word and go forth equipped with the power to do. Remember God is a God of Love, Compassion. The Good Shepherd will bless and give you Love; all life will sense the aura of your soul powers.

"Here the disciple takes his vows. Thy Master shall instruct you, until in full you sip freely of the Holy Grail. Cast out all fear, say in a loud voice: 'In the name of Love, begone all negative shadows, all false appearances. Let clarity and strength of mind and body be mine. So mote it be.' Bow thy heart upon the life of the Rose, and ask that you arise a new person, reborn in the White and the Golden Flame of the Christus. Let your blood flow warm with the Love of the Rose flowing through you and out to all life.

"Yes, disciples, let this spirit be thy prayer as you await your greatest initiation. To each in a different way will come the glorious blossom of the Path. Obey what is told. Always let three days and nights be spent in supplication, foregoing all earthly pleasures. (Meaning), remain at thy altar even in the midst of all thy objective activities. If faithful your Star will be given you. Arising from your vigil, you will come forth an Adept of the Path.

"All your innate desires must first be laid at the altar of the Rose and Lotus if you would reap the 'well done' of the Christus. Then in Akasha will one enter the Table of our Lord. There flashing from the Christus' hand will be the 'Cup of the Grail.' Even so, Blessed Mary, purity supreme, will call out: 'Behold my Son. He is the Way, the Truth, the Life of all mankind. In, through and by him ever live the illuminated of the Rose. Saints, Angels, the Hierarchy have their conclave here at the Inner Table. Come, mankind, enter the mystery school within. Brave the crucible of Gold. Know first-hand my heart of Love beating for all humanity, understanding your woes. Reach unto me, Mother of the Christ Babe. As you do, even so you reach to God, the Son and Holy Ghost. Ever do I intercede for you.'

"Even as we heed her words, joy will ride the morning winds. At the zenith of some noon hour one's heart will leap into its esoteric harvest. As you receive give back. All nature will serve you who are a greater servant. Heed all that is given in the Golden Flame, for potent is the message depicted from the Eternal Flow.

"At the Immaculate Table where ever sits the Christ, come in reverence, bow down and listen. Hear Him say to each disciple: 'Thou art whole, go forth in peace. In thy heart sing like a bird of the morning skies. Fight not, but live in brotherhood straight, eternally young with the nectar of the Absolute for thy nourishment as well as nature's abundance. With gracious deeds and thoughts cover thy walking mission. Laugh much and hurry not to gain temporal things. Rather ever hunger for the divine in all life.' "

Now I did with Master H ascend in consciousness in Cosmic Light. Master H pointed out a mighty Book suspended in triangular form. The All-Seeing Eye from the apex gazed down upon it.

"Behold, Pensatia, the Book of Love. From center of the Godhead flows this Book down to earth for all mankind to read when able. The pure love signature shines like a golden jewel for all humanity. Here are the written records of all true mating sealed by the Pentagram proclaiming the Alchemical Marriage. Only through the Flame of

White does the disciple have the power to read therein. From this infinite scroll all immortal books are inspired and brought forth on earth. Love alone is the great instigator of everything. . . . Look," directed Master H.

Turning, the pure gold for a split second almost blinded my vision. Then, in a cool blue spray of dew mist, my soul consciousness lifted to a white and Holy gate. All fell from me save my cape of white, which I wrapped about my naked self.

Gone was Master H. I stood alone on the citadel of the Book of Love in the Flame of White. Fragrant rose petals fluttered through the cosmic air. The Book flew open. "Read, Pensatia," echoed in the distance the beloved voice of the Master.

At first all seemed but symbols, which as I pondered upon became written words. (Afterwards the Master told me, by symbols first then by words, does the objective mind pick up cosmic truth). The inner signature of man, bird and beast and all nature was etched indelibly here. I desired to see my page and there it was, past, present and future. Some pages were closed, no symbols or word could I read. Only that which the disciple can face is permitted. What was revealed I kept in my heart, so I could ponder and study upon that received.

I discovered that if there was a rapport between one and others, it was possible to read from this Cosmic Book for others when they were unable to do so. Conscious clairvoyance became a fact here. The reality back of its three dimensions became plain. Only in conscious awareness does one feel the Love Rays pouring through the Flame of White for man and earth. Only in conscious oneness with the Father may we utilize our divinity. From this Cosmic Record, our cause and effect of life after life shows the eternity of the Now.

As our inner centers open we revolve with our divine signature. Thus only is Cosmic Illumination born for man.

Then our bodies obey and follow the inner Word. We are in reality living flames of light, life and love. All that is written in this fiat will be objectified. Here from this Book of Flame all gongs are sounded for the great transition. One keeps the body only as long as earth life is stamped on the infinite ledger. We can not change our hour of departure. Only the grace of God may impregnate past karma and grant a stay on earth. We ask and await the Father's will.

The exodus across the River Styx is the true democracy. All must meet as One here, King and commoner alike. Only the awakened and illuminated may by grace, if it be the Father's will, go beyond his alloted time. To live long on earth one must have in his blood and bone the divine mixture of the Elixir and Stone. The fabled Powder must impregnate the physical body in Christed resurrection. It must be liberated Light, thus regenerating the body in active acquiessence of immortality. The Golden Ray from the Flame of White must, from top to toe, be consciously experienced. When we ourselves become Love, then all that the Father has is ours. Love is the open sesame of the Holy Ghost.

chapter ☆☆ **ELEVEN**

Again I keep my vigil. Master H leads with candle flame my steps into the White. Within my heart is warmth, and love fire embraces my consciousness. I sit in esoteric fashion there in the White of Heaven's hearth.

"Pensatia," spoke the Master, "gaze now in the mirror of the heart and pen as you receive."

I did scan the cosmic lines upon the heart's scroll. I saw

a mighty train come streaming into port. People, one by one debarked, and in white robes came and sat with me upon the cosmic greenway. Always words formed beneath the symbol.

"People when ready rise in consciousness to Love dimension and settle on the cosmic hearth and receive ever as you. By meditation they absorb wisdom."

Now a second symbol revealed itself. A "7" in red fire was silhouetted in the spiral of Akasha. I felt a great and holy stillness impregnated in this "7". Again the print of Akasha rolled before my inner eye.

"All must become the sacred '7' before the heart reveals in full for them. All must partake of its inner quiet. Its spirituality must sing for all its calm, eternal music within blood, bone and soul, before the OM of God lifts the Veil of Isis.

"Not until '7' purifies and synthesizes all duality of Maya will the disciple realize the heart is his eternal home. It takes 7 years, 7 steps, 7 initiations, aye, 7 lives, unless by grace of God, to lift the mundane weight of illusion into the realm of the sacred '7'. When the pupil has so ordered his life and obeyed the discipline and lived from the heart's call he will surely gain the signature of '7'.

"No intellectual reading of esoteric books can inject the cosmic fluid of the 7th *sound, color, word* and *action* upon the disciple. One must by Soul Alchemy alone deserve and bring the peace and glory of the '7' within his consciousness.

"Remember after attaining the '7', one is quiet, dignified and fortified with the ultra spiritual key of this mystic '7'. Its power transforms and makes luminous all lesser things. It is the cosmic mother of numbers bringing softness and clear intuition to one.

"The inverted, unawakened negative side of 7 is depleting, weak and shilly-shally. Those with a 7 birth path must find the inner realm of 7, or they are lost in Maya's

illusion. The mandate infallible of '7' is: Find the inner
initiation of my number."

Now a silver star five-pointed formed against the cosmic
screen of Love in the Flame of White. It undulated in
vibrational quickness, like mercury.

"Silver is the quintessence of mutability. None attain
the Red Powder of the Gods, or the Alchemical Gold,
until the five pointed star of silver pours through one's
fivefold expression." So interpreted the symbolic star to
my heart's consciousness.

"Silver is the cooling fusion of love's all. Without its
balancing effect love's ardor would be chaotic. The signature of the silver star is ingrained upon all initiations on
the mountain top. It calms and lowers the electrical power
and cosmic fire of love into objective expression.

"Even those who wear only outward silver are more
stable than those who wear gold only. In all esoteric and
exoteric expression silver is imperative for balance. Before
Cosmic Illumination is attained the silver waters of Baptism must flow through one's interiors. All disciples must
partake of the silver drink. The silver star must be ingrained upon the rose center of the heart. By Holy Mary
and the Christus, silver heals and tempers, bringing firm-
ness to all it touches. It is the middle denominator of the
Way, soothing the paradoxes of the Way and liquidating
the froth and nonessentials of the climb to the Holy Grail.

"Christ attained the blessing of silver in Jordan stream.
Henceforth the essence of the five pointed star was His to
Crucifixion, Resurrection, and Ascendency in Isis. It was
the potent, adhesive power of the silver star of God that
gave Him strength to carry through and suffer. Always
God the Father gives to every disciple the cosmic and
mundane balance of silver.

"All gold has a base of inner silver to create equality of
essence. Ponder on this. Remember, all insanity, karmic
or otherwise, is caused by a lack of silver. The fires of love

must be tempered in the cool, steadfast waters of quicksilver, which, though ever running, is a benediction of fusion quality. As the disciple immerses in its silver flow, slowly but surely there comes a holy moment in the heart's altar when the silver synthesizing of the Way, emerges into the wholeness of the five pointed star. Then, and then only, does one know: the outer and inner are One."

chapter ☆☆ T W E L V E

My blessed Master came. Through the dusk of night came he close, and spoke:

" 'The Flame of White' is finished. Faithfully thou hast traveled and penned the truth as I revealed. Readers, ponder well. Other books shall be scribed by you, Pensatia: three times three, ere the New Age blossoms. All shall be published. And one you knew in long past lives you shall meet, and lo, he will bring to public view each and every manuscript. And the way will open, in all ways materially and otherwise, to publish them. So have I spoken. And even so, Pensatia, ever shall you be cared for; even so shall all spoken for you come forth. Even so he who sees that my works are published, I shall bless greatly cosmically and otherwise.

"Now I go. Several years hence I give you your first book to be published.* There will be times when it seems impossible the fulfillment of thy mission. Yet with faith and obedience, Pensatia, carry on through the dark hours even though ridiculed and crucified and all tangible assets

---

*"A Journey Into the Light" privately printed, New York, 1958.

dissolve. Daybreak shall come and the way shine like the sun upon the works I send forth.

"This finale, the 12th chapter, is short. Blèssed is thy pen, and blessed those who aid in the publication, and more blessed is the message within to every reader who ponders and heeds.

"Arise and enter the Path leading to the Flame of White. Thus will the Holy Grail be yours, and the influx of the Christed Man come forth. Even so shall my blessing ever be with you. Remember 'when the student is ready the Master appears.' Let this be *you* and *you* and *you*, beloved readers.

"Now I salute each and everyone with compassion and love and a deep understanding of all your past and present karma. Fear not to face the new frontiers of the New Age. With the tools of the alchemical secret of the Rose of Life, and the example of the lowly Lotus, arise and give birth to the Divine Cosmic Heritage which belongs to all Humanity.

"Now I, Master H, depart for the Highlands of the Soul, the High Mountain of which Pensatia shall write in the time of ripeness. This book has been in Akasha, in the alpha and omega of the Word, though only now does it objectify in print. Peace Profound to the whole wide world, to nature, and my beloved people."

. . .
. .
.

THE ROSE OF LIFE

PRELUDE

Into my earth pilgrimage walks the Master H.

As quietness steals upon me, in shade of tree, hotel lobby, or by cool of river, comes he, beloved Guru of my soul.

"Write," he speaks, in positive gentle tone. "Write of The Rose of Life. Descend with me into the cave of darkness and rise to witness thy birth of The Rose of the Golden Dawn."

He placed his hand upon my head, saying, "Blessings be yours, and unto all who find the Way and obey."

Music, simple, profound, resounded from my soul down through my heart and out to earth so green.

As quietly as he came, so went Master H.

Yet, with my pen will I follow and record this travelogue.

PENSATIA

Dedicated to Claire
in friendship and for a service
gratefully remembered.

Again, the Master came, saying, "The Rose of Life, would you know, Pensatia? Then follow me."

I arose and did his bidding . . . We started on a Path winding upward, over and through earth. I left all behind, bade farewell to all familiar landmarks. In simple attire, even as he came, I obeyed.

Darkness was, and my heart was sad, for home and earth looked bright, and all joys seemed behind, and the Rose so far away. Yet the Master's call, and the inner voice, was greater, more compelling than any earthly gain.

"Grieve not, Pensatia," spoke the Master, "you will return. They who seek the Rose, only travel that they may return with Holy Gifts and Sacred Graces. Now, keep heart and eyes upon the Path. One goal, one purpose: to attain the luminous petals of the White Eternal Rose."

Even as he spoke my heart grew lighter. Strength and a sweet peace stirred within me. I minded not the darkness, or that the winds bore harsh upon us—even when pain rent body and feet, following the Master through dimness and strange lands.

"Be not dismayed, Pensatia. The Path lies through all experiences: past, present and future. One only seems to have lost the familiar, while learning to see from the inner dimensions of cosmic reality instead of only objectively.

"When at the upward pinnacle of our journey, holding full bloom the Rose, then will all which bears one's signature be returned. There, in cosmic vantage point, one will know the glory, the victory of the Golden Dawn, that lifting of the mundane veil into the clear vision of the fourth dimension and above."

As the Master conversed, we were progressing slowly and steadily upon the Path. Plant, human and animal life became most interesting, since the Light of the Master's aura penetrated into all darkness, which made possible the communion with everything. Yet, in traveling, my body often felt weak, ill, and a great nausea fell upon me. Almost I cried out to turn back. Then it was that the Master did lay his hand upon my head, and bade me rest, and he did give me a green liquid, brewed from the earth's heart. Drinking, strength came to walk on.

"Always," explained the Guru, "the student who obeys and follows to seek the Rose, God and the Masters protect, heal, aid. When the going gets too rough, stop for a moment. Consciously let go, even of the Path. Then a sudden influx of Life will flood your being, and one is ready to take another step on the Path. Remember, obedience to leave all, to follow, to tread the Path, which is very dark at the onset, are one's credentials to the Rose of Roses. Dare all and you will receive all. For, at the summit, where the Path turns to golden hue, where the Holy Cross and the Rose blooms triumphant, white and most powerful, one will kiss and remember every step upon the Way as a precious birth into Light, Life and Love."

It was now pitch black, the road was rocky and my bare feet stumbled.

"Come, student," spoke the Master, "we bed for the night. Always must the Pilgrim of the Rose observe the Laws of Nature and God as they pertain to the physical body. Rest, sleep and food are requirements along the esoteric journey; as well as play, recreation, joy."

Even as he talked, the rough Path seemed a soft, soothing bed. Soft breezes, music, like unto a lullaby, sounded through green trees which suddenly lined the way. Dancing elves, beautiful forms of people walking to and fro, were seen. Our hearts and thoughts seemed to blend with them. Then, as I relaxed, I perceived home and loved ones. A closer bond was felt.

"You see," came soft the Master's voice, "how the Path, even at the beginning, brings a realization, a sprouting seed of peace and brotherhood. When the Rose thou hast attained, Pensatia, then will one be all things to all life—and life will be all to one. So, persevere, all who seek to know."

Oh, how blessed the sleep, if only for a moment, upon the Path of the Rose. All burdens seem lifted. One knows he has started the pilgrimage to the Holy Grail. Though weary, he rests with trust and faith that God and the Master are leading.

So it was. I awoke, and behold, the Path grew brighter. Lessons in slumber seemed to have been absorbed, as though through the evening hour, a cordelier had been handed me.

"Come," called the Master ahead, "we have a long way to go and much to learn."

It was a bright young morning and my spirit was high after the clean rest. Invigoration gave me stamina to obey. Taking hold of the Master's hand, we bore upward to the heights.

"Remember, Pensatia," spoke the Guru, "there comes many a time, before attainment, when I leave you on your own. Prepare for those moments, for, unless the disciple is integrated in the center within his own heart, the Path avails nothing but empty illusion and nonfulfillment. Yes, at certain periods on the Rosy Path, one must stand alone, even without the Guru's presence. So build strong and sure as we walk the Way together. Know, even when you see me not, in the shadows, I see, know, and ever watch the true student. When the student is ready, all Heaven, Nature, and the Hierarchy bring forth one's mission."

We often came to little hills and beautiful vistas. There we would sit and scan the earthly horizon. At such times he would point out the meaning of each stage of the ascent of the Rose. It was a most precious memory of the pilgrimage. Always gentle, yet firm of speech, understanding, compassionate, of mundane and cosmic virility, he made clear the search.

"Pensatia, never hurry or rush. All wisdom is born of great stillness and patience. Even in one's earthly duties, karma and Caesar's tribute—easy like, gently fulfill thy cause and effect. Clearing, pushing through to the center of even measure, take earth and heaven, else the lack of balance throw one to the abyss.

"Always have time to pause and refresh thyself at these hill-marks and sylvan oases. These happy interludes, if only for moments, keep the student equal to climbing the summit within to the transcendent Rose of Life."

Indeed it was so. The rolling green hills, the woodland trees, the clear rivers, made the Path more easy to travel and gave the student stimulation and courage needed to progress.

"Always," intervened the Master, "let vision and imagination and heart warmth tune all thy efforts. For earth alone brings misery and stagnation.

"Come, let us up now—for, see yon cavern? There must we enter."

He turned, blessing me, making the sign of the cross, and, igniting the light within my heart, he bade me in God's name and Holy Christus, to enter, and be not afraid. Trusting in the Master, I found the Path descending into a cavern, most dark, chilly, empty of music, beauty, or life. Not even the Master was visible, though I felt the presence of his hand on mine. So dark it was I knew not where my foot would tread. Faith and trust only guided me through the long darkness. A whisper floated to my heart from the Guru.

"In this darkness, Pensatia, keep your consciousness on the heart, then will a subtle light lead you in safety through the many such milestones on the Path.

"Privileged indeed is the student who passes this cave in the discipline of the crucible and wins.

"Remember, seeking the Rose of Life is no idle jaunt.

It needs all the twelve ingredients of the Elixir. At each cycle of the Path a portion of the fabled Stone is built into the awareness of the disciple. So fear not, nor despair. At every obedient tread on the Path, one is closer to the immortality of the Rose. When all seems lost, and in vain, a mockery, only *obey, keep on,* ever look within to God, the Master, and Nature to guide one to Cosmic Consciousness, which *is* the Rose of Life. Always one experiences hours of blackness, rough and stormy weather, when it seems shipwreck is the answer. *Remember then thy heart's light* and love will surely see you over and beyond the stress of thy cause and effect.

"See," pointed Master H, "already the Path brightens, becomes smooth, lighted with a glowing Star. This blessed symbol is ever seen by the disciple after passing through darkness."

I did indeed behold a lustrous five pointed star. It warmed and did cheer my heart as though bidding all to follow the Wisdom Path. I felt victory to come, felt a promise of my divine destiny. A deep gratitude born of humility was in my soul, for I realized that only by grace and the Master's presence do we go thus far.

"By one's efforts, too," spoke he. "Always remember, one *earns* the Master's touch."

"Yes, Master, I know," I answered, "yet these obstacles none could meet without their beloved Guru, who has attained."

Now, I did thank the God of all people. Lilies sprang in lush growth upon the Path—a fragrance filled the air about us.

"Purity of zeal and heart-prayer-thanks are ever symbolized by lilies on the Path." He plucked one and laid its whiteness upon my heart, saying, "Ever, students of the Rose, keep pure thy motives, thy steps, deeds, that one be worthy to give birth to the immortal Rose.

"At the beginning of the climb to Azùl, or Isis unveiled, one often hesitates to follow all the way.

"When earthly objects, money, friends, love, all seem to depart; when death often takes away those close—here is the crucial test. When barren emptiness looms, when supply is cut off, many cease and go back into material gain. Yet the true disciple climbs on and up the Holy Ascension; on with humble adoration, faith and prayer, through the discipline, the crucibles, to the transcendent finale of all his efforts, the conscious awareness of the Rose of Life. Ponder well, Pensatia, for temptations to leave come to all. Even as one decides, so is karma liberated and soul destiny brought forth. At any dimension on the Path—yes, even when almost at the top—aye, the highest sometimes fail, and the neophyte comes up front because of childlike faith, and willingness to learn."

chapter ✩ TWO

Now, on my journey to the Rose, I drank often of bitter waters, often undergoing servile and menial work. Often my pockets were empty, my living quarters small and ugly. Yet, the goal was kept in sight, and agreement was made with my karma. Even as through loss, sorrow, change, storm—in pressing on, the Master came; that is, I felt his presence, his watching, silent, yet flowing to me subtle strength in my mundane labors.

And when the night hour arrived in my room close to the stars and heaven sky, the Star would light my heart, and the Path would brighten, opening up like a cathedral window for me to see in a higher dimension; until, month after month, there came a moment in the midst of meditation when the Master H led me into the sacred fire of the Heart, where, after a long stay in its crucible, I passed the

first Holy Initiation upon the Path. Ever after a closer
relationship grew between pupil and Guru.

Now, understanding and meaning became alive in the
discipline. Meditating, talking with the Master, I learned,
little by little, to carry back to earth the wisdom garnered.

I ponder now on one of the precious, rare talks the
Master gave me in the Heart's Shekinah.

"Pensatia," so he spoke, "early on the Path students
must learn to transmute the lesser into the higher, and the
higher into the lesser until the two become one. Thus it is
the hardships, trials, grief—all steps upon the Path must
be Christed and flooded by degrees with the essence of the
Rose. Only as one does this can they be known as disciples-to-be. Here within the Heart live the sacred wisdom
teachings. To receive them, obedience and perseverance
at all costs, is the way. Every duty, action, thought, must
bear the stamp of the Master. They alone *know*, for they
have trod the Way and know victory—illumination
through self-mastery. To every neophyte walking the age-
old Path, are tests, lessons, duties given, needed to build
the Stone and the Elixir.

"No two students have quite the same experiences,
though the end in view is always Cosmic Consciousness,
or conscious at-one-ment with the Creator. Every student
runs afoul the cause and effect self-generated. That which
is weak and off-base from cosmic law must be transmuted
or liquidated at each milestone upon the Path. Thus only
can one progress. It is the Way to the Holy Grail, to the
shining Star, to the Christ Babe in the manger.

"Now, Pensatia, see what happens as one steadily ascends the mountain."

The Master pointed to a narrow, high trail winding upward on a towering mountain, so lofty, ominous, that it
terrified me. Down in a green valley I saw a thousand
lights, heard gay music and people enjoying gala times,
which echoed back to us.

"Come back," they called, "join us. There is nothing else save this."

The Path ahead loomed into misty darkness. Only a faint star glowed far on the mountain top. It appeared to beckon, as though whispering, "Have faith and follow the Guru. The God of your heart will not fail you."

"Pensatia," spoke Master H at my side, "choose now, you must. Each who has gone thus far can go back to the ignorance of the Wheel of Life. Yet, once you put foot on yon mountain trail, none dare, or does, betray the Master or the seeking of the Rose. One follows through, up to the breaking of the inner seals into consciousness in the Light. Even though all appears veiled in misty darkness, danger. Remember, Pensatia, they who obey and follow, letting Love and Faith be their only talisman, then shall God and the Masters protect and lead them safely through hell to the unveiling of Isis at the mountain top. Yet man is free to choose. As one dares, all heaven and nature aid him. What say you, disciple?"

I looked into his eyes of such deep wisdom. Shame was mine, that even for a split second the thought of going back had tempted me. "Disciple," he had said. Surely now, I must and I shall make my pilgrimage to the Rose. Let such be the prayer of all who have entered the Path, to be worthy of discipleship.

Then it was I bore upward with my Master, leaving all temporal things behind. A soft wind, rose scented, spiralled down from the starry heights. It seemed to make our footsteps lighter, seemed to bear a song of hope. Angelic beings, a rustling of wings was felt.

"Ah," spoke the Master at my side as we rounded a bend on the mountain ravine, "see, already the Cosmic Hosts bless us, as they do all who seek to pierce ingnorance with the Golden Dawn."

A peace and happiness prevailed within me, even while sadness lay heavy also upon my heart. Oh, to bear with us, loved ones and those who know not there is a Path.

On through nights, days, months we traveled ever towards illumination. Yet always did I bear in mind that all learned on the Wisdom Path had to be given back to earth, nature, and man. The journey was seemingly apart, only as a means to a glorious end: service to God and humanity.

"Always, at this stage, the student trails upwards alone and apart from wordly activities. Though liquidating karma and performing objective duties, one's inner steps seem to be isolated from the crowd. Ever it is so. The nearer the heights, most lonely and barren the Path appears, at intervals, to be. Austere is the scenery. Often only faith in knowing that beyond all obstacles shines the Garden of the Gods, immaculate wisdom, cosmic consciousness supreme. Yes, through the arduous discipline, loss, sorrow of the Way, glows at last the Holy Grail.

"Pensatia, there comes a growing peace, love, power to bless, heal, to serve gracefully each step upon the Path. Let us (each) persevere, know and remember, all who obey the mandamus of the Rose of Life are cared for; even when all supply seems not, the Lord will not forsake thee. Dig thy ditches. Ask, and it shall be; even when you have not, know you *have*. Often the disciple is ready to give up. Only the light and promise of the Masters gives one strength to go on. Thus, little by little, they gain the unfolding of the Rose within.

"Oh, yes, Pensatia, the night will pass. The glorious gold of the inner temple shall compensate for all hardships, opposition, and the letting go of mundane dross. So, when in dire need, be not afraid, for all belongs to the Lord. According to cause and effect, past and present, plus thy efforts to gain the mountain top—so will thy earthly wants be cared for. Yes, even abundance shall be thine.

"Now, behold with thine inner eye."

I did place my consciousness deep within the Eye of

Shiva. So did the Master with his Staff of Azùl, the Staff
of the Hidden One, speak the Word.

Then it was I perceived the crucibles. They were varied.
Different flames of color prevailed. A subtle fire seemed to
burn and mix with the toil and efforts of the aspiring neophytes. Every crucible seemed apart from the others, yet a
rosy beam linked all together with a six pointed star high
in cosmic heaven.

"Yes, Pensatia," spoke the Master, "all trials, labors of
humanity, are one in God's heart. Each bears the inner
signature of the Hexagon."

Everywhere I beheld disciples, neophytes and uncon-
scious workers on the Path. All hammering with the inner
tools, the Golden Key, within their crucibles. Some sang
with uplifted eyes and heart, working bravely to find the
living Rose and Elixir. Steadily, through the purifying
fires they worked. Others stayed in the flames only for a
second, half-heartedly they applied the Sacred Powder to
the crucibles. The transmutation seemed too arduous, too
slow. They fell away into the alluring outer life. Only at
pleasing intervals did they seek the crucibles. At the first
lick of the flames they depart. These bar themselves from
Cosmic Consciousness, for infallible Cosmic Mandate
states, "All must brave the crucibles to win the Rose."
Every step away from the crucibles weakens one's efforts
until all stamina departs. Yet all will have a chance in some
future incarnation to seek the Holy rites. God and the
Masters ever bless these weak ones, for once they too were
weak in some life. They know all will eventually become
Alchemists in the flames of the crucibles. There only gold
is made, and won.

"Ah, look upon the blessed over there. White-haired,
aged, withstanding in the crucibles, even when all dreams
seem futile, when love, home, money, are swept away.
Watch these patient, steady ones. In the ebony
night they toil in the burning fires of transmutation.

There in the alchemist shop I did look, saw old men, women, bent, and etched with sorrow, pain—yet upon their faces beamed a hidden peace, a smile of mystery unexplainable, only by the Holy Grail.

Suddenly a rose mist, a dew, arose within their crucibles and they brought forth a shining key of pure gold, and even as they did, age left them. The marks of their toil, the fire of the crucibles went out; only a luminous white light covered them. They walked forth victorious with the Elixir and the Rose. They *knew*, they *gave*, they *served*, henceforth, each an Alchemist in full regalia and power— the Word, become a living force.

"So must each and all stand within the mystic crucibles and win. No Master, God, or human, can conceive the Key of Life for one. You, she or he alone, only, can bear or build this Esoteric Key to the Immortal Rose. There is no way, except through the alchemist shop, through the fire of transmutation. God, the Masters, all nature aids, protects, guides, at given points. But faith and obedience and one's efforts in the crucibles, alone bring victory. Never seek to escape man's divine destiny. For though eons may pass, all will, must, in some incarnation, face the inner crucibles of the Philosopher's Stone.

"Remember, you who brave the storm, the dark, hunger, torment, the seemingly empty results—stay on. Know, when you least expect, gold will come forth, for use, service and love.

"Yes, Pensatia, it is inevitable that from the Holy crucibles comes Life, Love, wealth and health beyond one's dreams. Yet, remember, when all is given, share it with nature and man; horde it not, even for a day, thy gold, else it will vanish and be no more."

Now did Master H shut off the vision of the crucibles; shut off, he did, our journey.

"Go back and bathe more in the duality of Maya. Yet

keep in thy heart the essence of what is given thee. Until we journey again I bid you farewell."

I turned to speak. The Master was gone. I did obey and did mix in the hustle of earth, and behold, it seemed only a golden part of the whole.

chapter ☆☆ THREE

Now, after absorbing and giving back to earth what was received and learned upon my esoteric journey, again I traveled within and up to greet the Master H. And he did take me to a cool, pine scented mountain top overlooking a green valley. A waterfall trickled from the rocks.

Behold, Jesus the Avatar, stood tall, serene, against the background.

"Sit, and listen," my Master spoke.

I obeyed, and Jesus, the Christed One, did bless me, saying, "Pensatia, heed my words. Write from this vantage point."

An angel tall did stand guard, and rose fragrance filled the air.

"This is my retreat. Here I live and breathe the air of the Absolute. Here the winds from cosmic garden blow over me and upon my feet. Here the heart-fire of the Word flows through me and down to earth vibrations. Here I listen, hear and answer all heart prayers spoken with faith. Here I counsel, prophesy and heal. Always my heart is open to the least of humanity. I ever long that consciously man find his way here.

"Speak, Pensatia, ask now, and it will be. Yet ask for others too, else thy asking be in vain. Ask not for temporal things first, but for grace, wisdom, health, love, for, without these all else is empty."

From the depths I asked, and behold a star flashed forth a rosy glow.

"Yes," was whispered on the cosmic breeze, "for all who ask."

"Fear not, Pensatia, and all who reach me here, doubt not, for all that is asked here *will be*. Let not dismay enter thy heart if delays appear. For the answer often arrives over a dark road, and when a great heaviness catches the heart. Realize that when one has asked the harvest is, only the objectivity seems slow."

Now purple tints filled the air on the mountain top. Up from the green valley below toiled a neophyte. With valiant heart he trudged the rugged Path upward. Only the Rose and Lotus guided his steps onward.

"Often from here," spoke the Avatar Jesus, "I flash my image. Love, a word is given, a thought sent, to aid when they obey the Path. Their Teacher and Guru I send to them when they have prepared themselves. Never is the seeker of the Way left to bear his cross alone. The Father is ever with him. In every initiation to high degree the Cosmic steps forth and lifts one across the Astral stream into the pure ether of the White Brotherhood. Only when one disobeys cosmic law and order of the discipline, or *forces* his way through the veil, is there danger.

"Watch, Pensatia, see the potential disciple ever approaching nearer his divine destiny and sanctuary."

Far down upon the Path winding up to Pilgrim's Rest, the weary traveler toiled ever upward. Invisible, perhaps, yet ever at his side a Master walked, watched and strengthened his efforts. Now and then he caught a tangible glimpse, and he bore upward with renewed faith and love. Even though all earthly wealth, home, and mundane joys seemed gone. A star ever beckoned and a voice within whispered that all would be returned at the mountain top.

"Yes, Pensatia, keep faith. Here where I stand serene

beneath the pines of Allah, the Himalayas, far from earth strife, lies the answer to all who seek the Holy Grail. Remember, within the cup of sorrow is also the cup of joy."

What peace, what comfort, these words from the mountain top! Oh, to stay on the heights, away from earth strife, sorrow!

"Alas!" spoke my Guru, seeing my unspoken thought, "only the Masters may abide here. Yet, the disciple, if faithful, in obedience to the Path, may reach this Shangrila in meditation and soul projection. If their desire is pure and their mission can be furthered by coming here, physically, in body, or, if certain powers are to be needed in one's work, then, if karma permits, the way is opened for a stay in flesh with one's Guru. This is by grace, not by will of the student. Yet all must travel by soul flight and know by the awakened third eye the atmosphere of the Master. One must, through the heart, bathe in cosmic waters and sit at the feet of Jesus and learn what is his cosmic role. Here great healings take place. Here Jesus hears and lays his blessing of health and plenty upon all who ask in faith. Never does man ask in vain. If No is the answer, by law of compensation transcendent strength is given to bear, and always, if one does not rebel, a victory and cosmic blessing comes and in time the very No turns into Yes. So, despair not; all who ask here beneath the pines of the Himalayas receive. If all seems not, give thanks—know, when least expected aid will come—love, healing."

"Why, beloved Master H, even though one knows the truth of here, yet when back to earth vibrations, often, it is as if all were a dream?"

"Have faith, Pensatia. Remember all that is told above will be below. Seek not the time. Be at peace within. Be ever patient. Suddenly a new door opens, supply comes, health blooms, regeneration takes place—outwardly. It must be if thy Master and Jesus have so spoken. Nature, all the elements must obey, protect the trusted disciple.

Ask from the throat center, stand in the Golden Flame, drink of the white water of Azùl, and that which is asked will come forth."

A peace beyond compare fell over me like a beneficent mist. We were caught up in cosmic splendor. It was as if body and mind were transmuted into white light of infinite knowing and fulfillment. The song of the spheres poured through my being. I knew without a doubt all travail, all paths lead finally to this Holy mountain top where Jesus stands with open arms to welcome the weary Pilgrim of the Path. If one has found the way here while in the body, death cannot close the door. When transition comes the disciple finds death is just a clearer consciousness of his realization while on earth. To sup with the Masters is the goal of the Mystic Way.

Now, upon the mountain, beneath the pine of Allah, Jesus the Avatar did offer us most Holy bread and wine. Even as we did partake a mystic fusion took place. We knew we were sipping of the Holy Grail. We arose as knighted disciples with cordelier blue and golden staff. Yet, through the lowered vibrations the ageless song of the spheres echoed back from cosmic dimensions and the candle of the Rose of Life glowed warm within our hearts.

chapter ☆☆ FOUR

Again, with the Master, we raised our consciousness to the pine of the Himalayas. There we beheld a circle of disciples sitting on the cosmic green of grass. Tall stood the Master, silhouetted against the Golden Flame of Life. Every disciple received a smile, a blessing.

Turning to us he bade us enter the circle.

"To all here I will give a word that is needed to bring forth for them the Rose of Life."

We opened our inner ears to receive the cosmic lesson. The Christed One did walk the rounds of the circle of twelve. All received.

"Arise now. Obey that which was told thee."

I arose, filled anew with realization of divine blessings.

Now we walked away into the mountain fastness, into a remote glen. Sinking upon the grassy earth I wept for myself and all humanity. Nature, the wee ones, all the plant and animal life worshipped with me and cried out for the ignorance of man.

Now, in solitude I stayed away from the Blessed Ones, from the Master Jesus and the Guru H. I needed to ponder upon all my experiences. Health, wealth, love and perfect self-expression was not, as yet, objectified. In my heart, faith told me the infallible law—as above, so below —would bring forth. In one Holy moment I realized, defeat, loss, illness, all crosses transcended and transmuted into the everlasting Rose of Life.

Yes, all nature bore witness with me to the regenerating waters of life, as they flowed by with silver sparkle and power personified. Into the whirling waters, alone, in naked soul consciousness I bathed in its vibrational current. "Be still," as the Master had taught me, I whispered to the rushing waters. Like a placid mirror they were still. Laying my body upon the earth I did dip my lips and drank, and behold the image of the Christus did appear upon the waters. A voice sounded from the depths: "As you behold my image in all things so shall Love bless, sustain and feed you. The Christus is the infallible mark of cosmic consciousness, the golden stamp of truth. The Christus realized by Krishna, Buddha, Zoroaster, Jesus. It is the divinity shining deep within the heart of man. Only when the disciple becomes aware of the Light within himself, can he sense it in others. To become 'aware of the

Light' is the goal of the Path. All waters of heaven and earth hold my immortal flame. All elements drink from my heart, the Holy Grail. Only the Resurrected Christ can roll away the stone guarding the Rose of Life. Through Maya man walks within to find his immortal self. Only by obedience to the ancient Path of the Masters, by childlike faith, can the Holy Grail be won. In the sunset of the pilgrimage, when mundane shadows whisper of the silence of the evening hour, often, comes the pinnacle of illumination. Not often in the virgin steps of the neophyte, but at the seemingly 'last mile', it is then, if the disciple's heart still dares the upward climb that suddenly a great dawn rises from the hush of the storm, the trials. A curtain is lifted and behold one *knows* all which preceded cosmic awareness, is illusion, self-created. One realizes Light, Life and Love has always been his to claim."

Now the voice did echo as though from a vast distance, yet it was soft and clear within my ear.

"Peace Profound, Pensatia. Ever behold the Red of Rose from Holy Cross."

Drops like woman's tears fell like heavy rain upon me, there in the heights of Ra. A vibrant current stirred my being, sensitizing all my centers. The outstretched arms of the Christed Jesus did seem to gather all life from earth close to his heart. The Word, cosmic music of the spheres, lifted upon infinite realms a mighty crescendo.

Again, Master H calmly stood at my side and cover me he did with golden cape, counseling thusly: "Fear not to penetrate the strata of the Gods, leave all behind, save thy complement in man."

Now upon the altitude of Rose and Lotus a wondrous sight was seen—the fusion of man and woman into the immortality of Love. Saw I earth and heaven as one. Saw the miracle of birth. Golden light from the wedding of the stars. All heaven bore me up to my Bridegroom, for the last words spoken were, "I am yours and you are mine and we both are one in the Lord."

Before the Beloved voice had faded away I was again on earth soil. Master H had vanished. Yet on mundane air lingered a scent of lotus fragrance. A bird sang in nearby tree, as if in song to say, "I too have witnessed Holy sights."

Now a new steadiness centered in my living. I felt purified and ready to travel on with my Guru. All earth work took on a brilliant aura. Everything was a happy task. I thought, how gracious the Word, the Divine Plan. What a privilege the Path of the Rose! Every cosmic dimension earned must be lowered in service to humanity, must be lowered so that worm, leaf, waves of sea, are one with the disciple. What is gleaned above, must be repeated on earth. Love is the blood circulation of God's heartbeat, and so it must flow through humanity.

Ever in our midst, though invisible to the masses, move the White Brethren, those of the White Lodge and Golden Dawn. Yet in ignorance man cleaves to earth only and thus passes by the romance, the Path of Elixir and everlasting life. Yes, within our hearts is that Upper Room.

When night came, and sleep, a joy caressed my soul. Tomorrow, with the first break of day, I would again travel upward with my Guru.

So closes the fourth chapter.

chapter ☆☆ FIVE

Much sorrow has come to me—I who seek the bright summit of the Path. I who would see my Master face to face and feel the golden dew upon my body, have slipt. For a moment the Rose was forgotten. Earth illusion seemed all. And, as always, when one knows the law and keeps it not, the effect was great in price. But as the prodigal son I ran in tears to my Father's house. Behold, from afar He saw and welcomed me, forgiving the stumble, and did say, "All that the Father hath is thine." In white and purple was I gowned, and upon my heart was placed everlasting love.

Again on the Path, sadder yet wiser, I pressed forward to illumination. And behold the God of all people did give me supply, running over for my journey. And Master H did come and say to me, "To all who slip, all is forgiven. Thou art whole. Remember I too, aye, all the Masters on the upward climb, even as you, have fallen from grace. But always they arose and did tighten their cordelier and, forgiven, they climbed anew to Azùl, to the White Brethren, to the Christus of the Holy Grail."

Now the Master did lead me to a rose garden, among green trees and grass. A clear stream ran through.

"Relax," said he, "drink in the fragrance of the rose."

Obeying, I sat upon the soft waving grass. Great trees shaded us from a sun brighter than any light of earth. Lilies floated by on the running stream. Birds sang. We were indeed in some heavenly paradise. The Master sat near me, and did thusly speak:

"Remember, Pensatia, a thousand times one may negate the Way, yet, if truly repentant, all is forgiven and one starts again upon the Path. The Father understands all earth cares and will fulfill the heart's own needs. So rejoice and drink this Elixir and rose wine. Its delicate pink essence will renew and give one strength to follow the Light."

Reaching out with grateful heart I did sip of the Master's liquid. Gentle peace and soothing filled my heart. Old pains were gone. Old debts wiped out. Gold was in my pocket, my pure desires came alive to meet me. I knew indeed God is Love and Life everlasting and that all is One.

"Pensatia, when you go back to earth vibrations, take

the rose Elixir with you and sip three times three, until thy
body wields the strength of Isis, and even so of earth. Soon
a gate opens for thee, it wends through earth roads and
riches, yet within, its source is born. Heed not what others
tell thee, obey and write of the Rose of Life. Thy words
will live and light the valley for Pilgrims of the Mystic
Way.

"All is given, remember, O readers of the Rose, when
all seems taken away. All is attraction, vibration and
awareness. Have faith and absorb the law. The Word will
break forth. Always the lesser envies what it doesn't understand. Those who dare to stand in the Golden Flame
are above the law of the sweat of the brow. Those who
know this, be humble, give thanks and share thy bounty
as it falls on thee. For they who know the Father's heart,
all is health, wealth, love, and perfect self-expression.

"Remember, Pensatia," came the Master's words, "within, and without ever speaks the Word. Know, on earth
must heaven harvest be. As one lives in super consciousness, so will all materialize on earth. Heed not old wive's
tales or racial negations. Know the law of Life is Abundance. No Master was ever poor. Only through the discipline and karmic night does duality and lack seem. When
we emerge into the Light of soul awareness we attract what
we need. We have access any time to the Father's bounty.
So now let us travel onward to the inevitable summit of
cosmic awareness."

The Master took my hand.

"Come. We toil with joy the upward way. Kindle thy
heart's candle. Be not afraid."

Within the center of my heart I placed my consciousness. Then it was a door opened. We did find the Holy
Grove of green on the mystic Isle of Samos. An amber
light softened the atmosphere. Everything had a clean
fresh tang. A feeling, rather than a seeing, of a vast ocean
surrounding us. A fusion of the elements seemed to take

place, a foursquare union of earth, air, fire and water. We were indeed in a new dimension. It was as though the very essence of Life flowed as cosmic electricity through our bodies, rejuvenating, illuminating.

"Here," spoke Master H, "in this sacred Grove of Samos the disciple rests. One's wounds of travail are healed. He views the crags yet to climb. Under these tall green trees the comfort of cosmic truth is felt, walking hand in hand with nature.

"In the peace of Samos, with the Master one grows sturdy for the climb again. Often a great pain, weariness, penance, sears the heart before the door opens, leading to this occult grove of tranquility. Here all are measured in their cosmic value. The reality back of earth vibrations is shown and taught the disciple. Here the pure spirit of the Holy Grail is revealed by the Christus. One realizes earth and nature are reflectors of the Word. Only man has distorted the vibrational coil of matter. The disciple must learn to synthesize all points of the Triangle into the Hexagon, then Solomon's Seal will shine forth in all its glory. Often many lives pass before one reaches this Isle of Samos, in its green splendor within the Heart's Flame. Here the Rose and Lotus become an objective reality. One learns the poise, the steadiness of eternal signatures. Here as never before the Master stands in the shadows, watching, aiding with cosmic law the disciple to free himself from his karmic dregs, enabling him to cross into the Light of the Mountain Top. It is a beneficent grace and blessing well earned which crowns the disciple now. Consciously, or sometimes in slumber one absorbs higher teachings of the Masters. One, if fitted, is given lessons, experiences needed to bring him into his work or mission. Before one leaves this Grove, one knows his Holy orders and is ready to obey and do. A physical rejuvenation also takes place. It is good to be conscious, objectively conscious, while here; yet, often, one arrives here only in his soul body. Either way, a great initiation is enacted here on the Isle of Samos. Here the Master aids the disciple to gain strength needed for all his outer and inner forces."

Yes, it was true. Night and day I tarried here with my Guru. Earth life became sweeter. Blood and body circulated more life. Heard the Master ever saying, "Obey. All will be." Saw the Star of Heaven beckoning me to follow. Yes, how Holy the Path! Its ruggedness, pain and sorrow, now was transmuted into Gold. All that seemed gone, now came back, for the cosmic reality was seen. Yes, as I obey and write this book, The Rose of Life, each day is blest. God cares for me and ever I feel akin to everything.

So ends the fifth chapter.

chapter ☆☆ **SIX**

Now the Master bade me arise and face the East and the rising sun.

"Behold," he pointed, "the Flame of Life beyond."

Even as he spoke I felt the Golden Essence of Life flow through the sun disc and all my heart was aglow for the love of the Rose.

"Stand ever in the Gold. No harm or lack can touch they who, even though things seem not, stay in the Golden Flame. Ask what ye will, it shall come to pass, if it be the Father's will. Here, what is thought, positive or negative, is objectified. Very few earn the right to draw the Sun Dew upon themselves. Yet, all walking the mystic Path must attain the Elixir behind the sun. When once attaining the Flame of Gold walk not out of it, for it is life, and more abundant life. As one stands, sleeps and walks in it rejuvenation slowly and surely takes place, and power on all points of the Triangle. Yes, high beyond the sun disc flows pure the Word from God. Here the Holy Ghost, the Dove, flows out to all ready, in sublime initiation. It is only through the Golden Flame that the Stone and fabled Elixir is attained. Herein is all the physical refined and transmuted into one's body of Light.

"So, Pilgrims of the Rose, give not up when thou standest in the Flame and yet darkness prevails. Know O valiant student, blessed and Holy is thy travail. Thy Master, aye, all the Cosmic Hierarchy stand therein, watching, aiding, sweeping aside at climactic periods, all the illusions of Maya and stress of negative karma. This happens only through grace of God and the Master.

"The disciple knows not the exact time his cross will lift. Only know, there is a time when all that has been denied the disciple now comes forth—money, health, love, and one's holy orders. Yes, come it will, the harvest. Yet, often before, there is dearth, hunger, loneliness, often illness. Death seems near. Yet remember this, Pilgrim of the Rose, no matter how old biologically, those who stand in the Flame of Gold *will be rejuvenated*, have wealth, love, and their mission revealed. Their complement in affinity shall come forth, aye, and the two shall wed. Even though past ties prevail and separation by land or sea—two souls meant to meet will, at the epochal moment, be united on the Path.

"Yes, when all seems not, know it is. All debts will be liquidated. All appearances of illness leave. Even now I give to all who obey the drink of Gold itself. Drink three times a day. Drink and speak the Word from the Heart. Sip long or drink at once, it matters not. This drink is most potent to bring forth. When drinking say, or right after, *'It shall be now* in the name of Jesus the Christ, not my will but Thine O Father. Let power to do, to give, to love; let health, wealth and my divine mission now come forth.' Then be at ease, and feel the Flame, the Drink doing its Holy work."

O wondrous grace, O wondrous words of the Master, spoken on Isle of Samos. I drink, sip, and speak. Behold I know we live and find the Rose in the center of our hearts. *There* is the Elixir and Stone.

Now the Master H did point upon the cosmic horizon.

"Behold the vast expanse of Akasha. Thereupon is etched the Alpha and Omega of all that is or will be. Look and see your future, which is also your past and present."

Obeying, all seemed black, then misty symbols, pictures, formed upon the cosmic screen. My heart read with ease. My third eye quickened. The glory of the Rose blazed forth. Akasha unveiled past cause and effect and pictured forth the harvest of the Golden Dawn. Yes, there on Samos and up the spiraled Path we came to the leavening heights of the All. Here, beast, plant, earth and heaven and man were seen in their vibrational signature. Here the numbers of all were written. The great organ of the Gods pealed forth. Turning to Master H my soul spoke in silence to him.

"Blessed Guru, God of my Heart, blessed Mary, angelic hosts, give me true vision, true hearing, that I may pen The Rose of Life."

I heard my Master speak.

"Pensatia, it is written in Akasha. Behold, and read."

I turned my eyes upward. Aye, The Rose of Life, all the blessed mysteries given me, were seen finished and brought forth for all to read who would.

The Master laid his hand of power and comfort upon my head. All the Love of the Christus poured upon me.

"Pensatia, all is not in vain. Obey, for when God's time is ripe, the harvest is—my work. Then you, my amanuensis, shall live. My Light shall vitalize all you pen. Obey and write, my witness of the fourth dimension and beyond. Now close this chapter, walk to the green valley of earth, but carry back and pen all received."

"Yes, Master, by God's grace I shall."

The Rose of Life! What a challenge!

The Master came, saying, "Pensatia, consciously or otherwise, East, West, North, South: to the Wisdom Path, to the Rose of Life.

"Come, let us journey now that narrow Path, leading straight up to the immortal cosmic light. There is no turning back at this stage, only forward, upward, within. Now it may seem one is thrown back into the snarling arena of Maya. It looks impossible to climb this narrow pathway to the stars and Elixir and the Garden of the Rose. All that precedes this last lap of the journey seems futile, even the Master a myth. Yes, Pensatia, all earth pulls at the disciple. Heaven seems far away. You gaze up. All is mist, winds and crags. Down in the green earth all is pleasant, familiar. It seems to cry out not to leave the last landmark."

In stern voice the Guru now spoke.

"Free choice now is the student's. As one decides so is written one's tomorrow's. I leave you, Pensatia. If you dare to travel yon narrow pass and seek the Holy ingredient needed we will meet again somewhere around the spiral to the goal."

"Master!" I instinctively called. "Master! Stay!"

Yet he had departed before my thought found voice.

A great darkness and loneliness shrouded the Path. A sickness rolled within my stomach. I felt to flee back. Only a stirring within my heart, a potent memory of my Master's touch, caused me to hesitate. Could I fail the Guru? Give up when he had trod the Path—and won? What matter, save the Rose of Life? Try I would. And in the heavy dark I groped and found the trail.

Little by little I gained ground. Ever the Light of the Rose glowed down and lifted my heart in courage. Nights passed and morning in the valley of the earth came with the seasons. And still I kept to the rugged Path. Often was heard the growls of the beasts of the wild. All the sting of the elements bore down upon me. The heat of the fire of initiation sought to annihilate me. I noticed now a lilting fragrance in the air, an essence of attar of roses, or that subtle scent of lotus, while lofty music inspired my efforts to climb the narrow mountain pass. I had no earthly luggage, food or drink, just my consciousness, my urge to dare, only inner faith that somewhere up the trail my beloved Master would meet me. A shooting star whispered Hope. Suddenly a great sickness came upon me—a weariness. I lay upon the mountain trail, that rough terrain so sacred to the Pilgrims of the Rose. A soft touch covered me with warmth. I fell asleep, knowing in waking new strength would gird me to follow through. In my slumber my Guru spoke.

"Fear not, disciple, that which you need will come. Let go of all. Fear not the dour moments, the lonely hours, empty pockets. Keep on, steady, patient, loving and forgiving. Your pockets will be running over when least expected. Give thanks if only for a piece of bread; lo, it will blossom into plenty. In all darkness sleep, work, smile, for the Rose and Golden Dawn must come for all who persevere."

So upon the Path came a new day, came the brightness of fourth dimensional horizon, came the White Horseman over the hills of Shangri-la, came he fast, yet tarrying for a moment. He gave me a look, a beckon. I knew it was a token, a blessing, that all was well there in the "awaking." . . . There in the new day I did arise and taste of the green of nature, list to the bird of heaven, to the music of the spheres. Light as thistledown I arose and did make steps within and without to the mountain of illumination. Joy profound did race through my being as I climbed.

Far down in the valley of earth a cry of lament echoed up to me, a cry of great hunger, making me realize all that is received within must be shared with humanity. Traveling upward time seemed not. Duality left me. The paradox of life leveled into oneness for the first time. Perception of near and far, deep and high was revealed as a whole. In relativity a vision was seen of the end in view. Pilgrim's Rest wafted winds of welcome. In patience and wonder I took each step. And the grace of God did lead me.

Again snow came, spring melted the ice-filled waters, summer warmed the Path, autumn lay naked the trees. Then it was, in the hush of the evening hour the Master came.

"Pensatia," he spoke, "as promised we meet. Not by chance, but by thy well earned efforts—and to all who reach this vantage point, henceforth know, I will stand in the fire of the Holy Grail and behold each step until you make your Mountain Top. Remember, even if appearances are illness, poverty; or even if death seems near, or if forsaken, and the Dark Night rolls over you, you will come through and regeneration will be."

Peace, confidence, walked with me with the Master's presence. Truly, all promises of the Guru are kept. What matter the Cross, Gethsemane, the dregs of Karma? I would follow through. Silence would be my power, my key to the citadel of initiation within the Heart of the Rose of Life. I turned to thank the Master. Lo, he was gone. Yet on the cosmic mind a rose pen flashed these words: "Forgive, love, Pensatia. All needs and measure running over will be thine, and to all who obey."

Flowers, most holy white, of delicate sweetness, fell in showers upon the Path. In the midst I beheld Jesus carrying his Cross up Golgotha's hill.

"Even so, Pensatia," echoed the words, "must all carry theirs likewise."

Now as this seventh chapter closes I sense the Master from afar, sipping from the Holy Grail. There in the pines of the Himalayas, standing close to the Nazarene. There at the table of our Lord, he did take sacrament with the twelve. A voice echoed back these words:

"Thus shall all disciples do in time."

Yes, the Path brings one to the mountain of the Gods and to the communion with their Lord. All who brave the ascent through the pass and bear the Cross, find here Resurrection on all points of the Triangle.

O Holy moment! to know the shining Drink, to realize the Elixir and fabled Stone! Even in sensing the vision, still, the Path was far up yet. So mote it be we all endure to pluck the Rose.

chapter ☆☆ **EIGHT**

Now a synthesis of the Way was built into blood and bone. One felt a lifting of any physical weakness. Felt power born of inward light carrying one closer to the Rose —illuminated. And ever the Master's presence was felt as he watched from afar. It was beautiful—regenerating— the Path, now. All nature was green, fresh with heavenly winds. Humanity touched my heart at every step. Birds, flowers, even the weeds of wild gardens, seemed to speak a common tongue. Burdens, lack, were gone. Only the yellow gold Path of the Rose and Cross called me with its infinite romance—every aspect of earth. The darkest night was now bright with my consciousness of the inner Light and auras of everything of earth. All people, Life, was luminous. The harvest of the long discipline and crucibles was coming forth. Tears of joy fell as in humble gratefulness I gave thanks to God and the Masters for the Love bestowed upon all who tread in obedience the Way. Now, in relativity, thoughts became objectified. I longed for water, and lo, my feet found a spring wherefrom to drink. When hunger came it was satisfied. The truth dawned of that esoteric saying of the Christ, "Seek ye first the kingdom of God, and his righteousness; and all these things shall be added unto you."* And, "Behold, the kingdom of God is within you."†

"Yes," echoed the voice of my beloved Guru, "as one becomes integrated in cosmic law he becomes the law, thus his *words* create. All now is seen in the Holy essence of the fourth dimension—the Inner Signature. No longer does the world or outer causes affect the disciple. Where before he moved by faith only now he *knows* and in knowing has the *power to dare and do.* As the disciple handles this wisdom and uses it for humanity, so does he ever near the mountain of Mastership.

"At this stage the vibrations are high. One sees and feels beyond and above mortal ken. Yet, ever down in the valley of the unawakened, the Light must be lowered to serve, and to speak the common tongue. Often one must forego the right to have, and partake of the lowly stables, that others might find the Path. Incognito one becomes. That is, he takes on the garment of those he walks among. Yet always, Pensatia, mark well these words: *ever within* he wears the *Mantle* of the *Initiate,* the *Disciple,* the *Adept, invisible* save to those of *like evolvement.* They go forth as directed, and where, to fulfill their cosmic mission. When God, the Lords of Karma, sound the gong, the Word is sounded forth for the obedient disciple and one is lifted into wealth, travel and love, according to one's destiny. Often now, to the masses, or the unawakened, one is accused of wasting time. One seems to be doing nothing of value. Yet, mark well, Pensatia, *if one obeys as inwardly inspired,* be it menial or creative, or 'just living,' so does nature and the Master's feed, clothe and

*Matthew: 6:33
†Luke: 17:21

protect. It may appear that I falsify. Yet, disciples, always out of the blue comes thy needs fulfilled."

Even as the Master spoke I sang within, for I knew all these blessed books given me would be published and go forth into the wide wide world.

With new zest my pen was dipped in fourth dimensional well. Yes, now the Path became more luminous. Strength and inner power registered within me at every step. It was as if a higher food, vitamins and minerals of infinite chemistry and vibrational value became supplement to my physical nourishment. I worried no more about supply, for always the Father opened the way. Assurance was mine that all I needed would come. All that mattered was to continue up the spiral to Pilgrim's Rest. What matter the years? I knew regeneration and the illuminated heart would come to every student of the Way when the sacred chakras opened.

Now, in traveling, even a spring burst forth, or Rose Dew sprayed over and through me from above, refreshing, impregnating cells, glands, blood vessels with the rejuvenating fluid of the Elixir.

It was noted the higher one aspires, the more was lifted earth elements, as if all was included in cosmic embrace. Ever was sensed the oneness of the All. Green of earth, blue and gold of heaven fused into glowing whiteness. A polarization equalized, manifested now at every step of the climb to the citadel of Ra, the Lotus and the Rose. Yet, even now, being aware of the clear sweet virility of the Path—even though darkness cleared, I realized there was so much yet to learn, so much to dare—before the Rose came forth triumphant.

The hard climb was not finished. True, my feet were secure on the jagged rocks. Yet, far above, the Star of the Magi glowed like a distant comet. Even so, in my heart I knew the reality was there. So, as a child, let one obey and follow through.

Now upon the Path came She, a woman Master, who, at intervals, comes to all disciples upon the mystic Path. Most beautiful was she. Dark haired and dark eyed and vibrant with woman's love. Tarrying for a moment, her voice spoke out to me.

"Pensatia, long ago my presence was made known to you. Never have you forgotten. Nor I. Now again I come to say: Fear not. All trials will pass. Health, wealth, love, and one's cosmic and mundane expression will now come forth. If it were not so my presence could not be now. To all I come when the time is ripe, and the need is great, nearing yon mountain top. And when the awareness of the Rose Bloom is felt. I come, speak, give to each what they have earned. What I say comes quickly.

"Pensatia, listen, and lay within thy heart my words, for *they will be.*"

I listened and treasured all her message, knowing even as she spoke so would it be.

Only when the Ma and Ra are united, relatively, in the disciple, can the woman Master come. She equalizes the harvest and brings quick results. Men and women both have the feminine Master. Only when the inner is about to be objectified, does she show herself. When she does appear what is spoken will be.

So upon the Wisdom Path, Cosmic words, etched alive upon my consciousness from Akasha's Library, I read: "All evolvement and progress runs in cycles, day, night, seasons. There is an appointed time for everything. A time for the woman Master to appear. A time for harvest. An ebb tide and a flood tide. Appreciate with reverence, both, and usurp neither's purpose. To do so is to deviate from the goal. Bear watching thy esoteric stars, for therein is read the sounding of the gong."

Now the woman Master came up to me, tarrying a momentous moment, saying,

"Pilgrims of the Way, and Pensatia, it will seem I speak

falsely or that I am a fantasy, and my words of worthless value. Doubt not. In faith know. You shall realize that which I have spoken. Nothing in time of finite holds my vision. From above come my words. So let not faith waver. Maya would seek to destroy my presence, my prophecy for each. Heed not. Dedicated now one must be. And obedience to all given is doubly required.

"I leave now. Behold all, the miracle of thy abundance. Give thanks that all is and climb high to yon bright star. Get heaven first and earth responds. Get earth first and heaven is lost. Meet the two in one and you are in the Master's realm.˙

"Farewell, Pensatia, and like-students of the Way. When my image flashes upon your heart know I am near. Ever will I aid, protect and ease your mundane road."

Smiling, she turned and departed high into the mist of the Rose Dew.

I felt a blessed glow where she had stood. Felt destiny was there, self-made, yet ever glorious when attained. Kneeling upon the grassy ledge leading up, and one with pilgrims everywhere, thanks rose to God for His grace and wondrous laws. And as with patriarchs of old, an altar was built, made of all ingredients found on the Rose Path. Dedicated it was to all who would pass this way. All pain, joy, tears were transmuted into one dewdrop of the Rose immortal.

After prayer I made ready to journey on, knowing those who found my altar would abide therein. So, in time, is built the Pyramid of the Rose. In God's time and man's efforts the Apex will be added, proclaiming the Cosmic Man come forth. O sweet was the essence from the altar high on the mountain pass, and higher, even, the vibrations as I traveled onward. And ever greater was the flow back to earth. Round and round I climbed the dangerous, narrow Path to the luminous Star of Light. Nearer and nearer came the golden breath of Ra. Now, herbs, flowers, their aroma, birds of rare and wondrous color, came upon my vision. And the song of the spheres rang throughout the Path. Small and steady were my feet. All the air of the Rose Dawn spiralled through me, washing one clean, in preparation for the great initiation high in the garden of vision.

Now people of wisdom, those of art, philosophy, science, letters, music, crossed my path. It was as if I made friends of all thinkers, past and present. It was most natural and congenial. I was treated as one in thought and goal. Their inspiration was a benediction. Yet in their exalted companionship I never lost kinship with those in the valley. In fact I felt more closely related, felt their hopes, sorrows, their chains of Maya. Love, compassion and a happy unity was mine now as I traveled the high ascent. Peaceful, easy-like, more stabilizing, earth and heaven fused—as one neared the top. All must fuse in equal balance, for, at the climactic initiation, all of earth we must lay, Christed, on the Altar of the Rose.

chapter ☆ **NINE**

Now I perceived in my mind's eye and awakened centers a new and Holy gate leading to the White Brethren. Tall, forbidding, they stood guard before the Temple of the Rose. Knowing one must enter to dare further, I made to open the massive doors, but was brought to a quick halt. I felt myself a neophyte. A lamenting tore at my heart. Had I come thus far only to fail?

"God," I made plea, "lead me now to thy sacred Altar, that the bloom of the Rose be known. May we break through the ignorance of our exteriors and open these doors to the esoteric Hierarchy."

Long fell tears. Heavy my pain. Time seemed eternity, and still the doors were closed. Austere, the White Brethren silently flanked the entrance, making no sign of hearing my plea.

"Yes," spoke from afar Master H, the beloved Guru of my journey, "as one ascends to Isis' Sanctuary and the White Lodge, when near the infinite doors of Akasha, naked one stands before the divine portal, realizing in one fell-swoop of awareness, the gap between them and the Hierarchical Host. Before admittance, equal polarity of finite and infinite must be ingrained on their credentials. No weakling, anemic student will pass to the exalted Initiation of the White Lodge. Many, reaching this entrance, abide life after life here, building their balance of polarity. For all which is not equalized must be, before these doors open. Soul, mind and body must become one unit. As above so below, as below so above, is the key. Never will the White Brethren and Angels three, guarding the Portal, open, until in degree, the disciple stands foursquare with earth, air, fire and water, fused in blood and bone with their body of Light.

"The cosmic edict is, heaven and earth, man and woman together must enter the spiral within these doors to the Garden of the Illuminati."

I turned, feeling admittance was refused, for, in aloneness I stood. My Alchemy Mate was not. Yet, even in making ready to leave, a flute bore music to my ears. Nearer it came, and with it came "he", wedded in triune affinity with me. As we greeted the wonder of the heavens rolled over us.

Behold, the great doors opened. Hand in hand we entered the spiraled Path to the Rose in bloom.

"Thus," spoke Master H, "must all, man and woman together pass through these doors. Thus must all duality meet and fuse as one before the Elixir and the Stone give passage to the Citadel of Wisdom.

"Yes, at the ripe moment of self-made destiny, when the sacred centers open, the Flute Call resounds far up from out the Mountain of Allah. And behold, the man and woman fated to the Alchemical and mundane marriage, must and will henceforth walk together to the Garden of Vision and the Resurrected Rose."

Now, as we traveled upward, a transcendent fire, gentle, yet enduring, strong, flowed through our being. Consciousness of complete oneness with my Beloved was mine. No words were spoken, yet our thoughts were one living flame. Nothing was hidden. We knew the goal of our meeting was the exalted Third Degree of the Rose, high on the Illuminated Mountain. There we would have the choice of our work, mission, Holy orders, et cetera. We knew all ascetics, hermits, monks, priests, in some lifetime must meet and wed their Alchemical Mate, thus giving birth to the Holy Grail.

"All who negate, or bow to fads, or continuous vegetarianism, or think to gain spirituality in denial will never gain entrance here or meet fulfillment. The middle way is cosmic law—right use of heaven and earth. As one thinks, so is he, truth infallible. The earth is not God but His footstool. Food is not the way to God, but God is the way to food. (Behold a paradox.) All is blest by the pure in heart. All is created in the divine image. *Hold to that in all things*, else walking the Path is in vain."

Now the White Brethren did hand us a bright green capsule.

"This is the cosmic leavener. All must partake who seek higher dimensions and live. Before space is mastered and travel to planets beyond earth becomes possible, man must discover this green essence—within, as well as outwardly, otherwise never can they reach Mars or Venus in earth body. One must earn this inner essence. By this capsule green the greater mysteries of air will be mastered by man."

As we tasted the capsule—it was more an absorption, and quickened our awareness of both mundane and infinite—a gong rang out. "Proceed, disciples of the Way. Yes, even as in nature, green is essential. So here one must eat of the emerald hue. One not ready for the higher green and who dares to sip this esoteric food will only be destroyed. Yet to the true and tested disciple it is beneficent, as is nature when loved. This capsule is green that one may know they are integrated and ready to go on. Otherwise you both would disintegrate before you made another step forward to yon white mountain.

"Behold now the Mountain of Life."

We looked upon a mountain so lofty and white, it drew us like a mighty magnet, yet our exhilaration was steady, healing, peaceful. There was a Path going straight up. Yet with ease we climbed or seemed to float, so light our steps.

Thus man and woman aspired together the ageless Path of Cosmic Consciousness. Color, song, wondrous scenery stretched from both sides of the Path. Angel wings flanked our boundaries, as though showering blessings. A fragrance, rose sweet, traveled with us. We were conscious of other like affinities climbing upward with us. Love pervaded the air. Far and high on lofty summit the Christus looked down. His compassionate eyes bade us come and sup with Him.

Continuing upward my Beloved's thoughts were one with mine.

Oh, that all could reach, attain the Alchemy Marriage! Bear the crucible, oh neophytes. Faint not, for yonder is the mountain all seek. It rises white within thy heart. Seek the Path, oh reader, again within thyself, to at last find the white mountain here. Pray God we all attain the Holy Grail.

Suddenly darkness shrouded the white light of the summit. A heavy fog made dark the Path. Holding to my Beloved's hand tears fell, pain came, where before joy had prevailed. All seemed fantasy.

"Come, let us return," I cried, "we have been duped."

Then we saw far down on earth people vivid and happy, heard their laughter.

"Look, it's there we should be, not here."

"Silence," spoke he, my love. "Know you not, faith has brought us thus far, and faith will penetrate this darkness. At every high step one must pass through a dark night. Let us persevere, as we have, in the long travail of the Path. This is only our challenge to another dimension of Attainment."

"No, no," I answered. "It is enough. Go back I must."

"You shall not," answered my mate. "Wielded in cosmic rites, together we go forward. Fear not, Pensatia, this too will pass. Suffer not this mirage to delusion us."

His words brought comfort to my heart. I was ashamed of my weakness.

"Chide not yourself," he spoke, reading my thought. "All grow weary as the summit nears. Let us lift up our voice in praise and thanks. Let us go on joyfully through this moment of night."

Even as we did, soon we perceived a beam of white light flowing from the mountain top, guiding us through the dense fog.

"See, Pensatia, what faith does? No matter, storm or stress, it never fails. Thank God for our blessings."

"Beloved," I spoke, "I realize why man and woman are fated to travel yon mountain together. May I give to you in some crisis as you have given to me."

He smiled. "You have, Pensatia, even though, often in the beginning it seemed unrecognized. It is written, 'Those of fated polarities give from cosmic garden one to the other, even if one or the other, objectively, is unaware of the interchange.' Always here in consciousness they meet and travel to the summit as one. It is called 'journey's end.' Yet we know it is only the beginning of ever higher dimensions of living. The vastness of God's wonder can only be learned by degrees."

Now the atmosphere again took on a rosy hue, and it seemed our bodies assumed and exuded a regenerated glow, as though the Elixir brought new life to organs, cells and glands.

Oh, to bring this experience back to earth! Words are so inadequate. Yet as we receive we must give in some measure.

"Remember," spoke he, my Beloved, "in all earth clay is found the divinity of the All. In nature runs the fiat of all cosmic law. On this sorrowing planet of earth man is initiated into the crucibles of soul alchemy.

"Forget not at the highest the depths from which one climbs, neither those who dwell in the valley."

Walking was bright now. All earth hunger, duality, was gone. We were nearing a far new country of cosmic vibrations. Our mind was clear with Soul Light. All was seen in relationship to the whole.

chapter ☆☆ TEN

Out into the ether. Up to the eternal quest.

I asked, "Is this what happens when death releases the soul?"

From the Master came the answer. "Yes, when one has attained cosmic consciousness in life, death is only the same, free of the physical, or the lifting of the body into its transmuted essence. If the interior senses remain unawakened, in death one is bound by such limitations, though certain progress is possible, if the desire to learn is zealous. Even so, the greatest growth comes in earth incarnations. The fiat from the Word is: Cosmic Illumination must be attained while on earth. All must find in some life the Path within and endure the crucibles. Gold, the Elixir, the Stone, must be made on the loam of earth."

It was becoming cold as we traveled upward. We now experienced a freezing barrier blocking our way. It was as if guardians of the Light were placing a mighty challenge, as though all hell and the Black Brotherhood of all negation, in guise of a raging blizzard, dared us to go further. I drew close to my Beloved. We bore through the storm which beat us to our naked skin. Stumbling we groped our way.

"Master, Master," we cried out together. No answer, only cold wind, icy silence. A numbness passed over our bodies. Only a faint glow far up shone upon us. Only faith kept our courage. An intangible strength kept us climbing "Roseward," to the heights. With the cold came quick night on the mountain pass. No longer could we see or feel the Path beneath our feet.

"We're lost!"

"No," spoke he, my Beloved, "God and the Masters still are with us, even though it seems not."

His words warmed my heart as an inner fire.

"Look," he said, pointing through the dark cold.

A light came from an open window high on the mountain bend. It seemed to bear an invitation. A rustic veranda overhung the rocks, giving an extensive view of a green valley. Just a glimpse, then blizzard winds and snow obliterated all.

"Yes," spoke my mate, "it is the resting house of Pilgrims on the Path, of which we both have heard. We must make it, Pensatia, and, by God's grace, we will, for there we must tarry, to rest and prepare for the ultimate journey to the Mount of Initiation."

Holding my hand within the strength of his own, we felt, rather than saw the Master's presence, touch, guiding us safely through the dark. Suddenly the cold and snowy winds ceased. We stood at the door of the wayside house. There, on the way to the Shangri-la of Soul consciousness, we gave a prayer of gratitude and did knock. The door opened. Behold, my Guru stood, broad shouldered, gray of hair, his massive beard blowing in the now soft, mellow air. Balmy breezes floated up from the valley below.

"Come in, and welcome, valiant disciples of the Rose," greeted us the Master H, his gnarled staff held strong within his hand.

Within a fire burned bright on a massive rock hearth. A broad, long table, Gothic, faced windows overlooking the green valley. A tall chair was placed at the middle facing the East. There the Guru sat. We sat on a bench, opposite the Master. We awaited his words. All wounds of the storm had vanished. Peace Profound filled the room.

"Let us eat first," smiled the Guru.

Even as he spoke, fresh green salad graced the board, bread and wine of clear sparkle.

"Eat hearty, disciples."

Surely, we thought, God supplies all needs, often in mysterious ways.

The Master sensed our wonder and made answer.

"To they who know the laws, nothing is a miracle. Yet, seek not the how or why now. Hunger must be satisfied and God provides, even at the last moment."

The food was good and rejuvenating, and quickly refreshed us. The wine had an esoteric flavor, or so it seemed. The Guru did partake also, though with moderation. We felt the power and healing vibrations of his aura, positive and radiant with his love and light. Just to sit in his presence was as a benediction. We felt the Christus overshadowing him. Yet he was most human and natural. Inner strength was revealed in every action and word. Amber light filled the room. Pleasant winds came softly through the window. A wild rose climbed up and peeked with green leaves into the room. Its fragrance lingered about the Master's aura, who then arose.

"Come, disciples, let me show you to your rooms."

Obeying we were given adjoining quarters, facing the veranda, revealing the sweep of the mountain top. We marvelled at the up-to-date conveniences—showers, lights, et cetera. The Master again smiled.

"If one knows the laws, all can be given for man's comfort, anywhere at any time; yet the lesser must be Christed before the Word obeys."

In rich simplicity the rooms were furnished. Soft greys, blue, with touch of canary yellow, was the color effect. In each room stood a flat-topped desk with mirror overhead, before which was placed a large comfortable chair. On the desk was candle and incense of sandalwood burning. A single fresh rose graced a small blue vase, embellished with Egyptian symbols. A single bed and bureau, early American, completed the furnishings with rare white throw rugs upon grey floors. All spotlessly clean.

We turned to thank the Guru.

He spoke. "Here Pilgrims of the Rose and Lotus, rest, renew themselves, meditate and gather strength to make yon high mountain," he pointed out the window. "By your own efforts you have reached this esoteric wayside house. Only those who obey and keep on the Path—in spite of all odds—attain here. Some in soul projection, or in dreams, a few in flesh, yet that is rare. Still, if one's mission is aided by coming thusly, God and the Master will make it possible. The lessons needed will be given you. Each will study alone. Even so, what is learned must flow one to the other and hence out and down to earth. . . ."

Now days went by. Nights and a myriad stars shone over the wayside house high on the mountain pass.

We renewed ourselves in the rarefied mountain air, acclimated our bodies to the alchemical challenge of the mountain top. We meditated within the heart's altar and wisdom from the Holy Grail was bestowed upon us. We toiled with new faith there in the wayside house and knew we were nearing the secret of making Gold and the fabled Stone. We knew when again we resumed the upward climb the pinnacle of the Rose would be ours in all its glory. In infinite dimensions we would receive our Holy orders. To know the privilege, glory and obligations presented there on yon mountain top would be indeed Life, Light and Love. Yet, even though we were affinities on all planes of consciousness, we realized Holy orders might again separate us bodily. We felt, however, that before this obtained, the choice would be ours to make.

Anticipating we knew not what, we sipped of the cup of happiness at this oasis of fulfillment, granted us during days spent in this haven in the remote Himalayas. Yes, that grand passion immortal of soul we experienced. And the wild rose climbing from the window sill, the soft valley winds bearing upward, seemed to bless our transcendent love. We knew the final rites, the Rose Wedding, would be consummated when we attained the Star of Isis on the Mount of Illumination.

Then one evening, when the cycle was ripe and the cosmic gong sounded, and the Lords of Karma spoke, the Guru, the noble Master H, called us to the massive long table in the room where we first had entered.

"Sit," he requested, "I would talk with you.

"Beloved disciples, in faithful study and happiness you have deported yourselves with infinite credit here. Now the time is ripe. Depart in peace and with new steadiness and inner strength attain Cosmic Illumination. And may the apex of the Rose indeed bloom for you. Here I watch, knowing all that happens. If you stumble, arise, and boldly climb. At yon mountain top you choose the glorious Third Degree, or the lesser, yet both are acceptable to the White Brotherhood and the God of all."

"So be it," we arose and spoke as one. And the ancient mystical Rosy Cross on golden cord was placed about our necks.

"Take nothing on this journey save your consciousness. Naked, gowned only with your heart's light and the Robe of the Initiates."

Even as he spoke we found ourselves out on the Path ascending on high. Though we were stript of all earthly garments we were not without apparel. It was fine, luminous, and of golden color. Weightless, these garments seemed to blend and fuse with our whole beings. God and the Masters, the very stars of heaven seemed to bear us upward.

How blessed, we thought, God's Love. How beautiful!

Now the vista ahead—all nature—made way for us. Though steep the Way now, a star of gold shone bright upon us from the mountain top. It was as if God, the Angels, and the Masters made preparation for our welcome. Distant flute music rolled down from the Pinnacle of the Illuminati. My hand lay warm within the comfort of my Beloved.

"Pensatia," he spoke, "no greater love than this, to travel upward, to Peace Profound."

"Yes," I answered with my heart, "great indeed is the grand passion immortal between man and woman."

Now night came, and on the hearth of Cosmic Path we slept in soft and gentle slumber. And Master H did come, in the silence of the night, flowing inner strength upon our interiors, that when daybreak should awaken us, regeneration would gird our pilgrimage.

And through the night old songs and loves of earth crept up and through our dreams, and cuddled close, as if to say,

"All is *one*."

chapter ☆☆ **ELEVEN**

Morning broke fresh upon the narrowing of the Way. We arose, fortified with the Rose essence of Dew, and did drink from the flask of nature as it brewed the secret potion of Ra Ma into our veins.

And now upon the Path came the hoary ones, the Venerables, the vanguard and custodians of the Way. They marched on either side, while swirling waters and thunder of darkness, the lightning, the dark currents and storm, all came to no avail against the phalanx of the White Brotherhood, protecting us upon the dangerous heights of Cosmic Consciousness. They neither spoke nor looked our way—the Hierarchal Masters—but straight they walked, as if to lead the Way. Even as we pondered, Master H's voice spoke directly, close within our ear.

"Give thanks, disciples, for, if the wall of Masters infallible did not protect the Bridge ahead no disciples could cross. For there the Black duality, the negative 'left hand' adepts apply all their arts and cunning to pull back the Pilgrims of the Holy Grail. But all who reach here, beyond the Wayside House, have earned the protection and service of the Masters. Have no fear, Beloved Ones, climb on, you will win and cross the Bridge—to Cosmic Consciousness."

Now, a sense of awe, an awareness of some stupendous occasion facing us ahead warmed our hearts. We heeded not the wild and subtle attacks of the Black Adepts. Even when we came upon sylvan meadows drenched with heavy sweetness of lush red and purple flowers, with sinister black clouds hovering overhead, drowsy music calling us to rest, intuition bade us keep on. We found our steps hard to take. Our thinking seemed dense. I felt my senses slipping away. Had it not been for the firm touch of my Beloved's hand upon mine, I would surely have sunk into the subtle allurement of psychic phenomena. Yet with every step victorious we gathered new strength, confidence.

Softly came Master H's voice through the cosmic mist.

"Never accede to the allurements of the Path. Never sleep in the in-between phenomena, else the Hierarchal Rose can never bloom for thee."

Now the Path led straight up, high and narrow. Single file now, we trod the ascent. In the near distance a White Bridge loomed. The one we were to cross. Silence reigned. Like a profound jury, we felt all depended on whether we were able to cross over the link between two worlds. No breeze. No Presence, save the consciousness of our goal— the Illuminated Mountain Top. We came suddenly and fatefully to the swinging Bridge of Light. We steadied our hearts with a plea to God and the Masters. Eternity lived in our consciousness. We stood there on the great divide, knowing if we crossed we would, for a second, know the whole of life, the *meaning* of the Path. All was dark, save the misty white of the crossing. No encouragement came. No music of the spheres. Not even could we see the Star upon the Mountain Top.

Suddenly my Beloved spoke.

"Here we part. Alone we must take this Bridge of Ra. Go in courage, Pensatia. Wait. I will meet you, when I, too, have made passage. If *either of us* lose our step—or senses—and are swept into the psychic abyss below, know we will meet and win in another incarnation. So let us say together, 'Memoria hominum tenear!' 'Let me remembered be!' We felt rather than gave embrace. Then in aloneness I walked the Way to the Mountain Top, walked steadily, strong in faith. The Bridge swung far and near, like unto a mighty earthquake. Earth and Heaven seemed to roll about me.

"Master, Master," I cried.

All my centers broke asunder with cosmic cleavage, and Light—blinding Light broke over me, and a great wind bore me across. I sank on a level of earth, yet, heaven

poured over and through me in White Light, more powerful than a thousand suns, yet the green of earth equalized
my polarity and I lay with a grateful heart, suspended in
cosmic dimensions.

And behold, again I felt the presence of my Beloved, my
complement in Man.

"We made it!" he exclaimed, taking me in rapturous
embrace.

Now, angels came and did bring us drink of the Elixir
and bade us rest there in the impenetrable land of the
Mountain Top. And there in what seemed an oasis of
slumber we sank in rest and the Master, near yet far,
whispered,

"Well done, disciples of the Holy Grail."

We awoke in the dazzling purity and essence of Light,
Life and Love. We stood together in the clarity of the
whole. And God and Hierarchal Masters, the Dove and
Holy Ghost was in us and about us. Our consciousness
was of earth, yet transcended, and was endued with the
living wonder of the Golden Dawn.

We were each adorned with a robe of gold, with purple
cordelier wound about our waists. A star, a Pentagram,
shone from our foreheads, while over our hearts throbbed
in fragrance elusive, violets, drenched in dew of Rose. And
behold, my Mate held a staff within his hand and I a silver
wand, and green buds sprouted all about. We felt alive
with power, and love flowed from our hearts' center down
to mundane vibrations. How profoundly peaceful!

We spoke together our thoughts, and behold, a ring
of gold circled my finger and a voice resounded: "THE
TWO ARE ONE."

Now, a touch, a presence, was felt. A hand upon our
shoulders, and Master H, the Guru of the Path, said:

"Follow and enter the Temple of Citation."

On the Mountain Top all became dark, black, like
wing of raven.

"Fear not. Walk straight ahead. Before every Holy Initiation or blessing one must, by faith, walk in the blackness."

And again the wind howled and all the tempters of the Black Brotherhood sought to grapple with our souls. But with the staff and wand held firmly in our hands, we bore onward, obeying the Master's voice.

"On and up, O valiant ones."

We heard rushing waters on every side. Lightning flashed. Yet, strangely calm, even in joy supreme, we made our way to Temple of Isis Unveiled. Yes, the Rose and Cross stood high at the entrance of Holy Pillars, upholding the Altar of the Rose. And our Guardian Angel led us within where a Shekinah blazed with virginal, everlasting Light.

We knelt and kissed the Cross, "The Old Rugged Cross," and from the center a Rose bloomed and behold —we were transfused and became one with the symbol.

And all Heaven opened, and earth, and all planets, and all nature. And Man was seen in the hollow of a mighty Hand. And a great Eye glowed warm and loving upon all.

And we knew ourselves to be standing in consciousness of The All.

Aeons seemed to pass, and all the "Sweet Mystery of Life," unfolded before us. We knew to ask was to receive. To seek was to find. And Heaven was within.

Then we looked in the distance along a hall, or corridor, with vaulted roof of blue and a million lights. At the end of this lighted corridor we saw a great chair, raised upon a high dais, and the Venerable One, Guardian of the Book of Akasha, sat within.

"Go," the Guru Master H said, "and receive your Holy Orders."

chapter ☆☆ TWELVE

We stood with hushed reverence before the White Light of the Mountain Top. A great sadness *and* a great joy prevailed within our hearts: joy that at last we bore witness to the Rose of Life: sorrow that all in the valley of earth were not with us. All the privileges, responsibilities, spoke aloud as a cosmic voice, saying, "All that is received must be given back. The Rose self-bloomed must flow its essence back to the valleys of humanity. Such are the Holy orders of all who seek the shining Holy Grail. Here in the Garden of Allah, the oath is taken."

The All-Seeing Eye bore upon us and Golden Flame in spiral form lifted us up to the Throne of Isis. There, male and female, two souls as one sat resplendent, crowned with Cosmic Consciousness. The Rose of Life bloomed triumphant from the heart and head centers, which met forming golden light from the Eye of Shiva. The Initiates of the Light arose and walked back to earth vibrations. Their mission was ingrained upon their heart centers. And all the stars of heaven smiled upon them.

Master H came walking out from Shangri-la and thusly spoke:

"You who dare the citadel of the Rose, be seated, and know your destiny high, where only the pure voice of the Hierarchy, the blessing of the Holy Ghost is available."

In this nobility of cosmic worth we pondered and weighed our thoughts. We had earned the presentation of our "orders." In our Heart's Altar the sacred fire burned high. Naught of mortal inception could pass this Infinite Degree. Only truth, hard won, awareness beyond and above the temporal could make the invisible visible. We sat, united in our oneness of goal, yet, in our wedded affinity we knew each to be complete within himself. We had earned the Love granted us, though now, by choice —outwardly—we might be parted. We knew ever we would inwardly commune, one with the other, through distance and space, bound by the law of affinity.

Now came the Venerable Ones, the Guardians of the Rose of Life. Came they with silver key, and a gold and jewelled one with scroll attached.

Each numbered: The Pythagorean Way, the Mystic Seven, the Celestial Twelve, the Karmic Five, and the Three of Expression.

Came He, the White One of the Hidden Rose, came He who watched and waited for Humanity's Initiation, two by two, on the Luminous Mountain Top.

Silence reigned as the blackness beneath the deep sea. Expectancy was king within our senses. Yet a new Peace Profound was ours. We sensed our journey back to earth. All mundane vibrations were seen in true perspective. A glorious service for the God of our Hearts awaited us on our return.

"Yes," I turned and spoke to he, who through the cosmos, by inner signature was my own. "What shall we choose? The earthly mating or that beyond?"

Our Hearts made answer.

"We go back together, yet in another life we will take a still higher Degree into the Rose of Roses."

Tears, like dew of the Path wet my cheeks.

"Master. Master H," my thoughts cried out loud, "without you there is no triumph. Blessed Guru, could I ring out one truth upon the Path to the wide wide world, it would be:

"The Masters *are; seek* and *find*. Obey and brave the crucibles and Gold will be. And the Rose will flower."

En rapport, my Beloved acquiesced.

The Venerable Guardian stood tall, commanding, before us.

"As you choose, so shall it be. Here, you bear witness to the inner signature of the Rose of Life. So, now, down yon Path back to earth. Let your light touch all who pass

your way. All earthly *needs will be met,* as you speak *in
faith* the Word.

"In this life, by choice, you will not enter into the
severance of all your earthly ties. Yet know, to God and
the Masters, each path of service is precious in the records.
Know, it is to the Disciples, the Adepts, and Devotees,
that the New Age looks.

"Here on the Mount of Illumination, the sum total of
the Way flowers for each. The Light is stabilized in consciousness within the center of one's being. Here in the
Holy stillness one is fortified and given daily 'orders' for
one's mission, or soul work.

"Remember, upon achieving this pinnacle of initiation,
the Rose of Life is yours to use at will, for the service of
humanity."

"We go," we spoke aloud, "within, to the God of our
Hearts."

And, arising, making the sign of the Rose and Cross,
we did turn our face from the Mountain Top and made
ready to descend again to earth vibrations. Yet, within our
Hearts we carried Peace Profound, and our Holy Orders.
Carried we Love, conceived and born from the crucibles.

Thus it is through Rose and Cross, through the Ageless
Way, one finds the Golden Dawn, and knows without a
doubt, THERE IS A ROSE OF LIFE.

.   .   .
.   .
.